©Minister of Supply and Services Canada 1985

Available in Canada through

Authorized Bookstore Agents
and other bookstores

or by mail from

Canadian Government Publishing Centre
Supply and Services Canada

Ottawa, Canada K1A 0S9

également disponible en français sous le titre,
Le Pénitencier de Kingston
Les cent cinquante premières années

Published by The Correctional Service of Canada
Under the authority of the Solicitor General of Canada

ISBN 0-660-11823-8
Catalogue No. JS82-37/1985E
Kromar Printing Ltd.

KINGSTON PENITENTIARY
The First Hundred and Fifty Years

1835-1985

Photographs and illustrations
courtesy of:

National Film Board
Queen's University Archives
Provincial Archives of Alberta
Saskatchewan Archives Board
Public Archives Canada
Kingston Whig Standard

KINGSTON PENITENTIARY

The First Hundred and Fifty Years

1835-1985

AUTHORS

Dennis Curtis   Andrew Graham   Lou Kelly   Anthony Patterson

CONTRIBUTING WRITER

Cecilia Blanchfield

GRAPHIC DESIGN

Richard Turgeon, WUFF Design, Ottawa

PHOTOGRAPHY

Dave Bryant   Mary Daemen   Richard Turgeon   Barry Wright

MANAGING EDITOR

John Vandoremalen

DEDICATION

To all those people - staff, inmates and private citizens - whose lives touched, or have been touched by, Kingston Penitentiary, we humbly dedicate this book.

TABLE OF CONTENTS

ACKNOWLEDGEMENTS

Over the years, many have shared the folklore and history of Kingston Penitentiary. People have been fascinated by it and have delved into some aspect of the life within its walls or have explored, in some detail, the many aspects of social life outside the walls which have influenced the rise of the penitentiary or had impact on life within.

It is an honour for us to be able to bring together some of their knowledge in this book. This is not a definitive history, but then it doesn't pretend to be. It is a story in words and pictures; it is the story of a silent, limestone fortress which has witnessed the birth and growth of a nation, has endured the changing winds of 150 years and still stands as a monument, separate and away, to punishment and reform. It is the story of the people whose lives touched, or have been touched by, Kingston Penitentiary.

The writing of such a book demands the support, the time and the effort of a great many people. We could not have begun this undertaking without the approval of Arthur Trono, Deputy Commissioner of the Ontario Region, Correctional Service of Canada. His kind support, bordering at times on the willing suspension of belief, made it possible to begin this work. We also wish to acknowledge the support and encouragement of former Commissioner of Corrections, Donald R. Yeomans, who so often motivated us to reach for what often seemed the unreachable.

We would also like to thank John Braithwaite, Deputy Commissioner of Communications, Correctional Service of Canada. John approached the project with the enthusiasm and goodwill that have characterized his distinguished career. Through his persistence and determination, this book has become a reality.

Halfway through the project, Mary Dawson became Kingston Penitentiary's 23rd warden. Without her kind support, abiding patience and forebearance, our research could not have continued.

Anne MacDermaid of Queen's University Archives and president of the Kingston Historical Society, generously gave material and encouragement to the project. Margaret Angus, noted author and historian of the Kingston region, its architecture and its families, provided a valuable review and willingly shared information and insights. The history of Kingston is a rich and varied one and Margaret helped us connect the life within the walls with the surrounding community with accuracy.

As with all books, the manuscript went through several drafts before it was ready for publication. Donna Eyre-Koen of Kingston Penitentiary gave us cheerful and patient help in typing and translating several types of handwriting and, worse still, undisciplined typing during development of the first draft. Special thanks are also due Linda Halladay and the women in the word processing unit of Prison for Women, who took the early drafts, edited manuscripts and marginal notes and entered them on their word processing equipment. The final manuscript was typed by Hélène Armstrong who worked long and hard at deciphering the last-minute changes to produce a professional manuscript.

Katherine Graham and Ruth Barton deserve a special vote of thanks for giving us their frank and candid comments in the first reading of the manuscript. Their editorial comments were invaluable in providing us with an outside and objective viewpoint on matters so often taken for granted by those of us who work in penitentiaries.

Perhaps though, none of this effort would have been possible without the initiative, drive and personal commitment of Murray Millar of The Correctional Service of Canada. Murray has been preserving documents and artifacts throughout much of his career, long before this was sanctioned or supported activity. Without Murray's personal involvement and persistence, our research would not have begun.

Dennis Curtis

Andrew Graham

Lou Kelly

Kingston, March 31, 1985

INTRODUCTION

TRANSPORTATION TO THE COLONIES

INTRODUCTION

The establishment of "Penitentiary Houses" was first enacted in 1779 in Great Britain, a direct result of recommendations by the famous reformer John Howard. By the time of his death in 1790 John Howard had achieved such renown for his exhaustive studies and detailed descriptions of the horrors and failures of the prison system of his day that he was honoured with the first memorial statue ever commissioned for St. Paul's Cathedral. Howard had been appointed Sheriff of Bedford county in 1773 and immediately began a round of inspections of gaols (jails) that took him further and further afield at a time when travel was expensive, uncomfortable and dangerous. The pestilential conditions and woebegone sufferers he depicted in his classic, **The State of the Prisons in England and Wales**, first published in 1777, immediately aroused public and parliamentary concern.

What Howard saw and described was the tail end of centuries of repressive cruelty that took life cheaply. Death sentences had been the way to deal with almost all crimes in England and Europe. There were about 2,000 hangings a year in England during the reign of King Henry VIII. Even well into the eighteenth century there were more than two hundred capital crimes on the books in England including, apart from the obvious ones, abducting an heiress, crippling cattle, cutting trees, letting fish out of ponds, sacrilege and stealing linen.

TRANSPORTATION TO THE COLONIES

Public revulsion against such extreme measures finally induced the courts to commute most death sentences to incarceration in prison or transportation to the colonies. America received some 2,000 convicts a year until the War of Independence in 1776, after which Britain established Australia as its primary penal colony. Canada also transported prisoners via England to the Australian state of Van Diemen's land, now Tasmania. Ninety two were sent from Upper Canada in 1838, and the practice did not end until 1853. It is not known how many returned to

Canada on the expiration of their sentence. Many did not. Prisoners who survived the overcrowded, disease-ridden journey, which could take the better part of a year on angry seas, were leased out as cheap labour to free colonists.

The fate of the transportee was bad enough, but prison was worse. The eighteenth century gaol was not run by government. It was a business. Gaolkeepers charged fees for the most basic services. Prisoners were put in irons that only bribes could remove. There were no public funds to feed prisoners. A convict with money could survive in some comfort. The penniless often enough starved to death, if they were not carried off first by typhus, known as gaol fever.

"A NIGHTMARE OF VIOLENCE AND SQUALOR"

What John Howard wrote about in **The State of the Prisons** was a nightmare of violence and squalor where convict gangs ruled and only the strongest had any hope of surviving. It was not a system which in any way addressed the reformation of criminals. It did not seek to

improve behaviour. It was geared solely to punishment and vengeance, verging on constant physical torture.

Howard's recommendations to the British Parliament called for special houses of penance — penitentiaries — in which criminals could be restrained from further offences and brought to renounce their evil ways. In these facilities for long-term, hardened prisoners, Howard called for a strict régime of sanitation, sobriety, coarse diet, "labour of the hardest and most servile kind, in which drudgery is chiefly required," and a "coarse and uniform apparel, with certain obvious marks or badges affixed to the same, as well to humiliate the wearers as to facilitate discovery in case of escape." Each convict would be obliged to serve one-third of his sentence in each of three classes in which the rigour of confinement and labour were progressively more moderate if his conduct and industry were satisfactory.

THE PENITENTIARY IN NORTH AMERICA

This idea for dealing with crime in society spread quickly to North America. In 1789, the first penitentiary in America was constructed by the Quakers in Pennsylvania. To the suggestions of John Howard was added the notion of solitary confinement. Cutting off communication with other persons was seen as a means of enforcing penitence, which would lead to reformation. At least this was the hope at a time when criminal behaviour was equated with sinfulness. It later would be called a sickness, and still later a disorder of the social environment, but the penitentiary would prove equal to all the theories. The bottom line was that society did not want criminals at large. Population expansion and an increase in crime brought a demand for more secure places of confinement. As the eighteenth century turned to the nineteenth, equally daunting prisons were built in other states of the new union. Closest to Canada was Auburn Prison, in northern New York state.

THE CANADIAN SCENE

In Upper Canada during the same era, the local gaols were usually quite inadequate facilities maintained by municipal funds. They were overcrowded beyond their means to contain or even control convicts sent there by the courts. As in England, capital punishment was an approved sentence for almost two hundred offences, but was rarely used. By 1841, after hard labour in penitentiary had been recognized as an alternative punishment, only murder and treason were punishable by death in Canada.

But it was the near state of rebellion within the local gaols that forced the decision to build a provincial penitentiary. On June 1, 1835, the Provincial Penitentiary at Portsmouth, eventually known as Kingston Penitentiary after the nearest town of any size, admitted its first six inmates. For a hundred and fifty years it has been one of Canada's major maximum security penitentiaries. For much of this time it was the only one.

"SEPARATE AND AWAY"

Kingston Penitentiary was built to be "separate and away" from the growing communities of Upper Canada, except of course from the one community it was located in. It was a significant departure from a concept of locally-based corrections. It represented a new world of confinement that removed the convict from his community and regimented his life. It introduced society to a new notion of punishment and reform.

Since its inception and long before, society has been trying to come to grips with the problems of crime, how to deal with it, how to

prevent it and how to reform the criminal. The penitentiary was built as one solution to the problem. It is not the whole solution. It was not perfect to begin with. It is not perfect now. The perfect solution to criminality continues to evade even the most civilized and sophisticated of human societies. There are only a range of imperfect solutions, of which the penitentiary is one. It has changed over the years, as concepts have varied.

THE TWIN DILEMMA

The story of Kingston Penitentiary reflects how Canada has dealt with its criminals, and even to some extent who its criminals are. Throughout its history, it has been confronted by the twin dilemma of penitentiary philosophy: confinement and reform. The penitentiary was built with thick walls and high towers to keep the convicts in. The local gaols were too crowded and too poorly funded to do this. Kingston Penitentiary's high

walls, regimentation and control of convicts came into being to ensure secure custody and confinement. That is why there have been so few escapes. That is why disturbances behind the silent stones seem so out of the ordinary and the mysteries of the daily régime excite such public curiosity.

People expect a penitentiary to hold inmates, especially dangerous ones, for as long as the court determines they should serve. Kingston Penitentiary has been doing that for many years. But it has also been dedicated to the reform of inmates. What that means has changed dramatically over time.

In the early nineteenth century, it meant meditation, penitence and reflection upon a life of crime. It also meant, in John Howard's book, a tight régime of control with hard labour at the heart of reform. We shall see the unrelenting zeal with which Henry Smith pursued this objective. Smith was the first Warden at Kingston Penitentiary, the first to be severely criticized by a public enquiry, and the first to be fired.

At other times, it has meant training and the introduction of personal discipline through work. Hard labour was a punishment but it was also a means of reform. As we shall see, Warden Ponsford in the early years of the twentieth century governed the penitentiary in the light of this philosophy. As concepts of how to reform criminals changed, so did the ways that the penitentiary approached its job. The use of social sciences to modify behaviour and attitudes represented quite a different philosophy of reformation, which reached its zenith within the walls when Kingston Penitentiary was a Regional Reception Centre in the 1970s.

FAMILY CONNECTIONS

Through all of these years Kingston Penitentiary has influenced and been influenced by the community it has served. The penitentiary's principal architect, William Coverdale, later displaced a Montréal architect to complete the building of what is now Kingston's City Hall. He also designed the Rockwood Asylum built as part of Kingston Penitentiary for criminal lunatics, as well as a number of the old stone homes of Kingston, many of which still stand today. On October 8, 1850, at a double wedding ceremony, the proud Mr. Coverdale would see his son and daughter married the same day to a sister and brother named Creighton. William Miles Coverdale married Jane Creighton, who died in 1865. Shortly after her death, William Miles was married again, this time to Fannie O'Neil. Their son William Hugh would become an engineer and company director at the turn of the century and assemble the William Coverdale Canadiana Collection of paintings, which has been published by the National Archives in Ottawa. Frances Coverdale made a particularly good choice in John Creighton. He would serve as Mayor of the City of Kingston from 1863 to 1865, and from 1871 until his death in 1885 as Warden at the penitentiary. Frances and John's youngest son, Robert Creighton, would follow in his father's footsteps and serve as Warden during the First World War.

Kingston Penitentiary's first surgeon, James Sampson, had led the council of the Town of

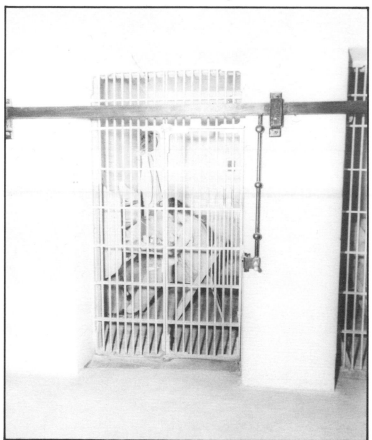

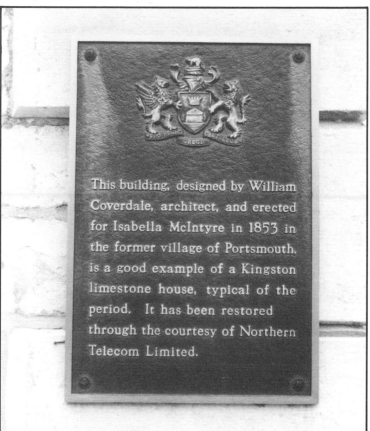

This building, designed by William Coverdale, architect, and erected for Isabella McIntyre in 1853 in the former village of Portsmouth, is a good example of a Kingston limestone house, typical of the period. It has been restored through the courtesy of Northern Telecom Limited.

flour and other provisions from the days the new market opened its doors. Ten years before the penitentiary was built, Kingston held about five hundred homes of resident families. Ten years after it opened, Kingston Penitentiary held almost

Kingston three times before it became a city in 1846. Dr. Sampson, who later criticized many abuses during the penitentiary's early years, would serve as President of the Kingston Hospital (the same building that housed the first Parliament of Canada in 1841), and was the first Dean of Medicine at Queen's University.

John Counter, first and frequent early Mayor of Kingston as a city, never received a salary from Kingston Penitentiary, but the records show that he was a steady purveyor of five hundred prisoners, all requiring food, clothing and other necessities. Not a bad captive market, then or now, for a provisioner.

It was not only the Mayors who became Wardens too, or the neighbouring Member of the Legislative Assembly, John A. Macdonald, who rose to the defense of a besmirched Henry Smith, or the Governors General who lived and too often died in the shadow of Kingston Penitentiary; nor was it just the family that ran the local tavern as a business but always kept a son on the penitentiary roster for security, or the children who were born and raised at the base of Tower Three in the centre of the west wall, or the tradesmen who found ways to profit within the walls: many Canadian families have touched or been touched over the generations by the hard, cold stone of Kingston Penitentiary.

Among those who had settled in the Kingston area by 1835, or indeed in the two Canadas (Lower and Upper, then East and West after 1841, and finally Québec and Ontario) which Kingston Penitentiary alone served for more than thirty years of intensive nation building, there were few who could have avoided association of some description. Perhaps a family member was on the roll of officers or among the inmates. Maybe it was as one of the thousands of visitors who have entered the gates through a hundred and fifty years, or as a consumer of penitentiary products, or as a supplier of some of the tons of goods consumed in the shops and kitchens each day. It could also have been as an officer of some

part of the criminal justice system that works its imperfect way to bring criminals to this place. Kingston Penitentiary has had, and continues to have, significant impact on the life of the community.

CANADA'S OLDEST PENITENTIARY

On the scenic shore of Lake Ontario, a long swim from Wolfe Island, within sight of the U.S. border, Kingston Penitentiary was built as tough to crack as anything on earth and has always been run by the best security team in the business. No one has been at it longer. Kingston Penitentiary is living history and tradition to The Correctional Service of Canada. It is equally a part of Canada's history, the place that has been designated and used for more than the life of the nation, as the

ultimate restraint for some of Canada's most dangerous and notorious criminals.

Because it has served so long as the main symbol of punishment in Canadian society, much of the life of the penitentiary might be cast in a negative light. Because it has carried from the outset the twin objectives of confinement and reform, it is important to understand how the interplay of these two objectives has proceeded within the high walls. This is a glimpse of the life of the penitentiary. It is not a definitive history of this complex institution. It is a selection of highlights from the story of Canada's oldest penitentiary and the community of which it is part.

The prison is closed and self-contained. However, like any society, it has established patterns of day-to-day life. While the public tends to focus on the spectacular escape or the murderous riot, it seldom gets the opportunity to see what the daily routine is, what convicts eat or how their lives are ordered. It sees little of the staff and how they carry out their difficult tasks with dedication and diligence. It seldom sees how the world outside and the separate, supposedly isolated, world within the walls interact.

This book is written on the occasion of Kingston Penitentiary's one hundred and fiftieth year of existence. Our journey will show both the dramatic and mundane. It begins, as it has for thousands of inmates, at the imposing North Gate.

CHAPTER I

HOW IT CAME TO BE

HOW IT CAME TO BE

The Provincial Penitentiary at Portsmouth was built and received its first inmates thirty two years before Confederation.

The idea of a provincially sponsored penitentiary was suggested in the House of Assembly of Upper Canada and was fully supported by the general public. As early as 1826 there was public concern with the problem of crime and a growing belief that existing sanctions were inadequate to deal with it. An editorial in the Kingston Chronicle of September 29, 1826, addressed the issue of the legal system and reflected on the need for a penitentiary:

"The cases which were tried at the late assizes at this place, furnish proof of the inefficiency of the law in its present state, and under existing circumstances. One man, for instance, was convicted for returning from transportation, to which he had been condemned at the preceding assizes, and though the Chief Justice, in passing a second judgement gave him no hope of escaping execution, the unfortunate being still showed by his deportment that he had no dread of suffering under his awful sentence. So little indeed did he regard the proceedings of our Courts, that it appeared at the trial that he had never left the Province after his first conviction. Banishment or transportation, for which, under the present mild administration of our Criminal Code the sentence of death for any offence short of murder is usually commuted, is not only in its very worst form no punishment at all, but is even, we verily believe, in nine cases out ten, entirely disregarded. The Penitentiary system, which has been tried in England and the United States, with good effect, although not yet with as much success as its sanguine friends had anticipated, would, if introduced here, be productive of essential benefit in checking the progress of crime. By rendering the punishment of offences real and certain, which is not, at present, the case, individuals would not be so reckless as they now are, nor would there be so many instances of repeated convictions of the same culprits."

Also in 1826, Kingston businessman and editor Hugh Thomson, Member of the Upper Canada House of Assembly, presented the idea of a "penitentiary" for the first time in British North America. It was not until five years later, when Thomson reintroduced the idea, that it gained full support. By that time the district gaols had become severely overcrowded. Their internal controls had broken down and escapes were rampant. This fueled public anxiety that crime was out of control. Thomson and fellow Kingstonian John Macaulay were commissioned to investigate the feasibility of a penitentiary. They reported back to the House of Assembly of 1831, recommending that one be built.

Thomson's monastic concept was markedly different from the purpose of the local gaol. These were places to hold prisoners awaiting trial, or where felons were to be punished. They also served as places of refuge for the poor and prisons for debtors. Criminal rehabilitation through hard work, silent reflection and religion, the conditions of confinement advocated in the 1831 Thomson/Macaulay report, reflected the reformist view. Their report to the Assembly was given swift approval. In 1832, £100 was voted to procure specific plans and estimates for the building of a penitentiary.

THE REFORMIST VIEW

Thomson wrote, "a Penitentiary, as its name implies, should be a place to lead a man to repent of his sins and amend his life, and if it has that effect so much the better, as the cause of religion gains by it. But it is quite enough for the purposes of the Public if the punishment is so terrible that the dread of repetition of it deters him from crime, or his description of it, others." It would introduce the concept of deterrence against a background of the collapse of other tools of punishment, such as banishment or hanging.

THE CONGREGATE SYSTEM

To obtain concepts for design, Thomson and Macaulay toured several penal institutions already in operation in the eastern United States, including Sing Sing, Blackwell's Island, and Auburn Penitentiary in the State of New York.

At Auburn they observed what was referred to as the congregate system. During the day convicts were made to work together at hard labour in absolute silence from dawn until dusk. They were then confined separately at night. Thomson and Macaulay observed the convicts eating their meals in a common room, seated in such a manner that they could not communicate with one another. They were impressed with this system. They rejected the more draconian Pennsylvania System (or "separate system" as it was sometimes called) in which inmates were totally segregated at all times. The Pennsylvania System of discipline had been developed by the Quaker community at the Walnut Street Jail in Philadelphia, which is generally regarded as the first true correctional institution in America.

They recommended the adoption of the Auburn model and the hiring of William Powers,

Deputy Keeper at Auburn, whose aid they had enlisted while touring that penitentiary. He was to design and oversee the construction of a penitentiary compatible with this system.

SITE SELECTION

The other concern facing Thomson and Macaulay was choosing a suitable location for the penitentiary. Two sites were considered: Hamilton, a day's coach ride west of Toronto; and Hatter's Bay, a short walk from Kingston, near the village of Portsmouth. Portsmouth had great quantities of good limestone available, to construct the prison itself, and to ensure adequate "hard labour" for the convicts. The location at Hatter's Bay on Lake Ontario afforded easy water access and transport for goods. The nearby town of Kingston offered a potential market for convict goods and the necessary supplies to operate. A British garrison regiment and a major contingent of Canadian militia were stationed in Kingston and could be called on in case of emergency. The penitentiary could serve as a military prison as well. Last but not least, both members of the Commission were Kingstonians. The scales were clearly tipped in favour of the King's Town. In the fullness of time (1952) Portsmouth would be incorporated into the City of Kingston, but long before that the penitentiary at Portsmouth was already being referred to as Kingston Penitentiary.

Thomson and Macaulay wrote in their report to the House of Assembly:

"After examining, with great care, all the grounds in and near the Town of Kingston it was found that no situation combining the advantages of perfect salubrity, ready access

to the water and abundant quarries of fine limestone, could be obtained nearer the Town than Lot Number Twenty, in the First Concession of the Township of Kingston which is about a mile west of the Town. The west half of this lot belonging to the heirs of the late Philip Pember, which contains one hundred acres of land reaching from Hatter's Bay, on Lake Ontario, to the rear of the first Concession, was accordingly purchased for the sum of One Thousand Pounds. The space between the Lake and Highway is about 15 acres in extent, of which nine or ten acres will be enclosed by the walls of the Penitentiary and on the west side is a fine Harbour, where vessels may approach within a few feet of the shore."

EARLY CONSTRUCTION

By the fall of 1834 the original south wing of the penitentiary had been built using local labour. There were one hundred and forty four cells, dark, airless cubicles with a bucket for waste and a thin bed hinged to the wall. Stacked back-to-back in five tiers or levels, each cell was thirty inches wide. Close confinement in tight spaces was seen then and later as an essential part of the penitential process. When new cells were built in four tiers in 1885, they had one and a half square metres of floor space, less than a toilet stall in a public washroom.

But the brand new jail stayed empty in 1834. The House of Assembly neglected to provide funds to feed and maintain convicts.

There were complaints about the cost, the British Whig lamenting that "£ 12,500 have been expended in erecting a huge, unsightly and unfinished wing of an immense building . . . all money gone." It was not an inconsiderable sum for the day. Given reasonable assumptions about conversion rates for currency and inflation over the many years since, it might be the equivalent of two or three million dollars in 1985. The estimated cost of the complete penitentiary as originally designed was £56,850, or perhaps thirteen million dollars in today's money. As an indication of scale, though, it is worth noting that the first-class warship St. Lawrence, with one hundred and four guns, had been built at Kingston twenty years earlier at an estimated cost of £300,000.

Small operating funds were voted for the penitentiary in 1835 and the first six inmates were received on June 1 of that year. They were assigned numbers, as all convicts would have to wear on their cloths and be known by. It would be more than a century before inmates would be referred to by their names. The six were immediately put to work completing the facilities that would confine them and tens of thousands of their successors.

THE FIRST SIX INMATES

Number 1 was Mathew Tavender, sentenced to three years for grand larceny. From the Home District, in the area of York and Simcoe, he was assigned No. 4 cell on the east side of the second range, south wing. Two days later he was put to work as a stonecutter, the first of thousands who would attack the hard Frontenac County limestone with sledge and chisel. He seemed to progress quickly at the work. He was made a mason on July 22, plasterer three days later, and on September 5 was promoted to bricklayer. He kept his nose clean, or at least he avoided punishment for a while. He was not whipped until August 30, 1835, three months after his arrival. He got six lashes then, along with John Hamilton.

John Hamilton was number 2. He would also serve three years, for felony. He became a stonecutter on the third day (everybody except the cook did "labour" for the first two days, while talents and tasks were sorted out) and remained a stonecutter in the quarries for the next two years. Then he got sick and was made a mason until he was released on April 18, 1838. He and Tavender were released together. Their joint whipping suggests that they might have tried to communicate with one another, which was strictly forbidden. Silence was the iron rule and deviations were harshly dealt with. These two and numbers 3, 4 and 5 were probably acquainted, since they had been sentenced the same day and were from the same district. Hamilton's cell adjoined Tavender's.

Number 3 was Edward Middlehurst, in for grand larceny. His sentence was five years, but in fact he was the first released. After working as the penitentiary's first convict carpenter for almost a year, he got sick in May 1836, and was moved from No. 2 cell beside Hamilton to No. 17 cell, 3rd range, east side. Whatever he had might have been contagious. He disappears from the roster after being ill for three months. Possibly he got a pardon, which was not an unusual way to deal with very sick convicts in the early days, when chronic care was an act of medical heroism even in free society. Better for the diseased to stay outside the walls, so that they would not spread sickness within. And if they were going to die, better that they die elsewhere. The penitentiary was not equipped to deal with death. It had no cemetery. But it had to pay the cost of a gravedigger if a prisoner died inside.

Also in for five years for grand larceny was John O'Rorke, number 4. He was the first to get lashed on June 15, two weeks after his arrival. He received five strokes of the rawhide that day, and six more on July 13. O'Rorke cut stone all his days at Kingston Penitentiary, and was never released. He died in prison in 1838, in the dark hours of a late November morning.

After a mix-up in the kitchen the first day, number 5, John Dayas was made cook on day two. It was an important job, for morale and health. He was given an assistant, 21 John Harris, in early September. But 21 only lasted two weeks before getting the lash and being put to labour. Then 45 William Riley arrived. He was made cook September 28, just in time to learn the ropes

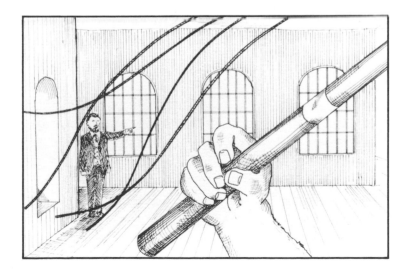

before number 5 Dayas, was given eight lashes and put to stonecutting on October 16.

When 45 took over the kitchen there were fifty six convict mouths to feed. He lasted quite a while, almost two years. But he was caught at something, perhaps pilfering, which is a constant temptation in any penitentiary area that contains goods or stores, and on June 10, 1837, was made a labourer and given seven lashes. Number 119, B.R. Snow, took over as cook June 12, 1837. There were a hundred and twenty seven convicts in the population, and more were arriving daily.

Number 6, the last prisoner admitted on the first day, caused the mix-up in the kitchen. Joseph Bonsette was the only one of the six who was not from the Home District. He came from Newcastle. He must have said he could cook, or perhaps it was assumed that a Francophone would have more flair for food preparation than the others. It was a mistake. After one day at the stove, 6 was made a stonecutter. He stayed in the quarries for a year, until he became ill in the summer of 1836, then worked as a shoemaker for the rest of his sentence. At least it was inside work. He was released in January, 1840.

THE POPULATION RAPIDLY INCREASES

As the population grew, arriving prisoners were set to new occupations and trades. They

were expected to build their own prison and, through their labour, provide life's essentials for themselves and sufficient revenues to maintain the institution and its staff. It was an impossible goal, never quite achieved, but not for lack of hard driving by the Warden and the keepers.

Number 7, John Endicott, did not arrive until July 8. By that time the administration of the new penitentiary had defined some needs. Teams of horses were being employed to haul stone from the quarries (later there would be a railway running from the pits to the pen). The horses needed shoeing. Number 7 was made the blacksmith.

Soon tailors were in demand to provide clothing for the growing numbers, particularly as fall signalled the approach of winter. Six convicts were detailed to set up a tailor shop on September 4, 1835. Three of them apparently were not suited to the trade, but 15 John Thompson, 28 Patrick Lamb and 29 John Edwards became the forerunners of a penitentiary industry that

survives to this day. Also on September 4, the first three women prisoners were admitted and started work as seamstresses, the most common occupation for females in Kingston Penitentiary until well into the twentieth century.

Number 9, John Parker, became the first painter on December 7, the same day that 54, Robert Matthews, would become moulder and 42, Sam Armstrong, would be named nurse. This probably meant keeping an eye on things until the surgeon came by on his round, which he did "daily at the appointed hour, excepting when necessarily absent from the neighbourhood." There was a hospital facility, but it was not easy to get into for two reasons. First, the surgeon believed that "were the hospital to be generally open to all on the surgeon's list, it might eventually prove a source of much inconvenience, by affording opportunities of concert and communication." And second, the hospital space was filled with the women convicts, who had been delivered to Kingston Penitentiary unceremoniously and unexpectedly and had to be kept apart from the men for reasons that were as apparent then as they are today (more on women in prison, Chapter VII).

Trades were inadequately but quickly filled as more inmates arrived in 1836. New arrivals seldom had any training for the jobs they were to do. Not everybody was cooperative. Many arrivals were resentful and rebellious. Attitude was as important as aptitude.

Someone had to look after the barrels for water and provisions. Number 18, William Freer, was made the first cooper January 18. Number 85, Keys Gleason, must have mentioned that he could use a saw for he became sawyer on the day he was admitted, August 24. The first wheelwright, 96 Lester Smith, started work October 1.

After a brief pause in 1836, when the government refused to allot further funds for construction, life at the penitentiary became a race to finish cells fast enough to keep up with the growing population. The wings stretched out from the rotunda at the centre — the Main Dome. It would be ten years before the walls around the complex would be completed, finally enclosing just under twelve acres. And the numbers grew. There were a hundred and fifty convicts in the prison population by 1840, four hundred and fifty by 1845.

CHAPTER II

EARLY DAYS

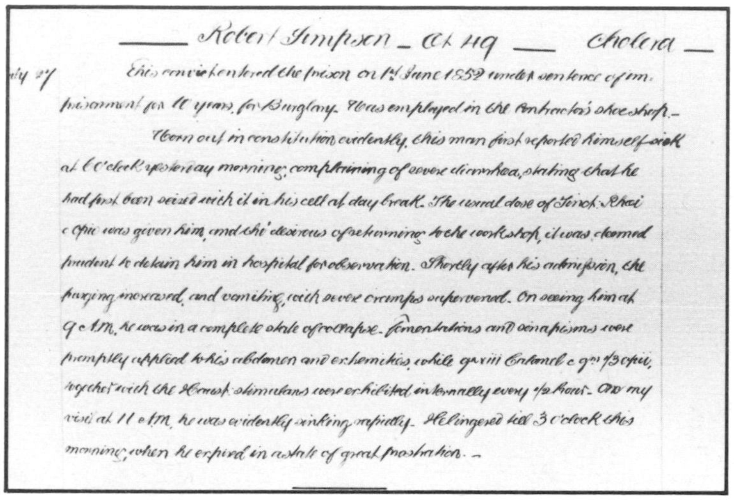

Robert Simpson — Ae 49 — Cholera —

[Ju]ly 27 This convict entered the prison on 1st June 1852 under a sentence of imprisonment for 10 years for Burglary. Was employed in the Contractor's shoe shop.—
Worn out in constitution evidently, this man first reported himself sick at 6 o'clock yesterday morning, complaining of severe diarrhoea, stating that he had first been seized with it in his cell at day break. The usual dose of Tinct. Rhei c Opii was given him, and tho' desirous of returning to the workshop, it was deemed prudent to detain him in hospital for observation. Shortly after his admission, the purging increased, and vomiting, with severe cramps supervened. On seeing him at 9 a.m. he was in a complete state of collapse. Fomentations and sinapisms were promptly applied to his abdomen and extremities, while gr. xiii Calomel c gr. 1/3 Opii, together with the Usual stimulants were exhibited internally every 1/2 hour. On my visit at 11 a.m. he was evidently sinking rapidly. He lingered till 3 o'clock this morning, when he expired in a state of great prostration.—

EARLY DAYS

Little attention was paid to the opening of the penitentiary in the local press. This is not surprising when one considers the news of the day. A cholera epidemic was ravaging the local community. Most Kingstonians were too preoccupied with their own survival to concern themselves with their new convict neighbours at Hatter's Bay. This lack of local awareness also accentuates the notion that the penitentiary was a place "separate and away" from the community.

The Penitentiary Act of 1834 authorized staff consisting of "one Warden or Principal Superintendent who shall reside at or near the Penitentiary; one Clerk; one Chaplain; one Physician and Surgeon; one Deputy Warden, who shall reside at or near the Penitentiary; and not exceeding twenty keepers to be appointed by the board of Inspectors, and to hold office during pleasure; and the Warden, Chaplain, Physician and Deputy Warden, to be appointed by the Governor and to hold their respective offices during pleasure."

In all probability Hugh Thomson, who had been instrumental in the birth of the penitentiary, would have been its first Warden, had it not been for his untimely death at age forty three, of consumption. His obituary gave testimony to the difficulties of life in such an age and climate. He left behind a pregnant widow, but had been predeceased by five children who died in infancy. The posthumously-born sixth child also died as a baby.

THE FIRST WARDEN

Thomson's place as Building Commissioner was taken by Henry Smith, who arrived in the colony in 1820 from Great Britain and became a prominent supporter of the Upper Canada Tories. He and John Macaulay paid this tribute to Thomson in their 1834 report: "If it (the penitentiary) should prove highly useful, which few can doubt, in the punishment and repression of crime, no slight share of the honour of its adoption will rest upon his name."

Henry Smith was subsequently appointed the first Warden of the Provincial Penitentiary at Portsmouth, a fact which was noted in the Kingston Chronicle. "Mr. Smith's habits of industry and active vigilance make him peculiarly fit for this responsible office." So too did his close association with the party then in power in the Legislative Assembly.

Warden Henry Smith was joined in 1835 by William Powers as Deputy Warden, and James Sampson as Surgeon. Rev. William Herchmer was appointed Chaplain in 1836. A Board of Inspectors was established to oversee the administration of the penitentiary, with John Macaulay as chairman. One keeper and one watchman were on strength opening day. Their ranks quickly expanded. At the end of 1837 there were eleven keepers and sixteen permanent and part-time guards on staff.

NO LIMITS TO THE INFLUENCE OF RELIGION

The chaplain was a central figure in the organization of the penitentiary. The legislation made him an "Officer" of the prison, giving a clear sign that religion would occupy a central role in the reformation program. In the annual report of 1835 the Inspectors pointed out,". . . as personal reformation to be permanent must be founded on Christian principles, so no system of prison discipline can be effectual in which religious instruction does not form a prominent part . . . there can be no limits to the sacred influence of religious impressions upon the hearts of even the most guilty."

Religion would be the last hope of hopeless cases for years to come. There were no criminologists, psychologists or sociologists. The clergy did the best they could to restore self respect and reclaim lost lives. Individual ministers and priests have been highly esteemed in the dual society within penitentiaries. For many years it

was almost obligatory to include a paean of praise to religion and the clergy in annual reports, as Inspector of Penitentiaries J.G. Moylan did in 1887:

"The highest importance should be attached to the labours of the Chaplains, since religious instruction is found to be the most effective means to make known to the convicts the principles of morality and to lift them up from their moral degradation. Many prisoners lose heart and fall into despondency and even despair, from which they find it almost impossible to raise themselves by their own unaided exertion. As a consequence they become callous and indifferent. Religion alone is capable of reconciling them to themselves, to society and to God."

There was to be no doubt about whose side the chaplain was on. His duties included convincing the prisoners of the justice of their sentence and persuading them to strictly obey the penitentiary's rules and regulations. Nevertheless, clergymen were to play a major part in the evolution of Canada's penal system from its brutal beginnings to its more humane present. More than one chaplain has been a hero to the convicts, helping to make their lives tolerable.

When St. Vincent de Paul penitentiary was opened in May 1873, a hundred and nineteen prisoners were transferred by boat from Kingston. The convicts were accompanied by their newly-appointed chaplain, a Roman Catholic priest who had come from Montréal to join them on their journey. He was Father Joseph Leclerc. Over the decade he spent as a convict chaplain, Father Leclerc established a reputation and a body of writing that brought him accolades in later years, including a tribute as "the first Canadian penologist." Excerpts from his reports were collected and used in the training program for officer recruits in the 1940s. His memory was enshrined in 1961 when a new medium security penitentiary was named for him, the Leclerc Institution at Laval, near Montréal.

THE RULE OF SILENCE STRICTLY ENFORCED

If the chaplain was the almighty's agent, the Warden appeared to believe at times that he was the almighty himself. From the start Warden Smith, with the enthusiastic support of Deputy Warden Powers, set about imposing a severe régime designed to reform convicts through reflection, hard labour and the fear of punishment. No sound of any kind was to be made by a convict except in the most exceptional circumstances. The convicts were alone in their cells at night, but were required to work together from dawn to dusk under enforced silence. They could not speak, look, wink, nod, laugh or gesticulate to anyone, except by hand signals to the keepers, and only then in connection with

work duties and wants. Gazing at visitors, singing, dancing, whistling, running, jumping or anything that might disturb the silence and harmony of the institution were forbidden under pain of severe corporal punishment.

Warden Smith proved quite adept at establishing the type of discipline within the prison that seemed to be anticipated in the debates of the legislature. His sentences, each one diligently recorded by hand in the imposing Punishment Books, ranged from six lashes of the cat-of-nine-tails for laughing, to bread and water diets "for making a great noise in a cell by imitating the bark of a dog." As well, the Board of Inspectors encouraged the practice of flogging for a variety of offences.

In the Brown Commission Report of 1849 the modes of punishment in the early years are outlined:

"From June, 1835, to April, 1842, the punishments adopted were flogging with the cat-of-nine-tails, and flogging with the raw-hide. These were the only punishments for offences of all grades.

"From April, 1842, to October, 1846, the punishments were flogging with the cats, flogging with the raw-hide, irons, solitary confinement, and bread and water instead of the regular rations.

"From October, 1846, to February, 1847, the cats and rawhide were suspended by the Government.

"From February, 1847, up to now, the punishments have been the cats, shutting up in a box, irons, solitary confinement in dark cells, solitary confinement in the convict's own cell, and bread and water."

Warden Smith imposed stringent rules to emphasize the retributive nature of incarceration.

The Brown Report recorded the routine. "Silently and obediently, day after day, week after week, year after year, the inmates at Kingston were supposed to shuffle along the corridors to their work every morning, their heads inclined at an angle that would prevent them looking at the man ahead, work all day at a bench without making the slightest gesture to anyone around them, shuffle to the mess hall and eat meals that were calculated to keep them alive without appealing to 'luxurious' tastes and not communicating with anyone."

A COARSE DIET

The food was intentionally routine and dull. The regular diet was published in the annual reports provided by the Warden to the Board of Inspectors. It looked decent enough on paper. On the plate it was a different matter. Keepers in the kitchen were ordered to buy the least expensive cuts and grades available. They usually took the dregs of the local market, which would otherwise be discarded as unfit for human consumption. The storage facilities were far from sanitary. Preparation was indifferent at best. Most meals came soggy and flavourless from large steam boilers. There were no condiments. Bread was the staple most relied on, and it would often enough be mouldy. At the turn of the century (1899) the Inspector of Penitentiaries, Douglas Stewart, put the view of the convict population when he wrote that "loathing is produced by the continuous and monotonous round of soups and boiled meats and the unbroken absence of roast and relish."

Convicts prepared their own meals, then as now, under supervision. Today there are qualified food professionals who work as instructors to guide the cooking. In earlier days such qualifications were rare in the kitchen keepers,

who were not there to instruct but to guard. What the keepers could do was to bag a pigeon from time to time, with a bow and arrow kept for this purpose. Pigeon was a delicacy for more than a hundred years. There is said to be an arrow still imbedded in a high beam among the rafters. It was not the only one to go astray, as the first commission of investigation into the penitentiary would discover. One notable kitchen keeper practiced for pigeons by using prisoners for targets (see Chapter III).

The most common crime for which both men and women were imprisoned was larceny (stealing money). Next was theft of animals — horses, cows, sheep and other farm and domestic animals were all listed as separate offences at the time. A thief might get only a year in jail for taking a pig or a cow, but a horse or an ox could bring a sentence of five years.

THE ALL-PURPOSE PRACTITIONERS

Staff surgeons in the nineteenth century Canadian penitentiary faced formidable medical challenges. Typically, they handled problems such as malnutrition, food poisoning, dysentery, scurvy, typhoid fever and lice. They had to protect the crowded inmates from deadly epidemics of influenza and smallpox introduced from the outside.

They tried to isolate patients with serious contagious diseases like tuberculosis and advanced syphilis. They patched up the victims of shop accidents and convict attacks. They dealt with alcoholics, drug addicts, imbeciles and psychotics. They examined new inmates, attended the staff and their families, delivered babies, pulled teeth and performed autopsies.

They usually had to do all this in dark, dirty, damp, cramped quarters without any assistance from antibiotics, x-rays, lab tests, effective anesthetics, specialized equipment, trained nurses or sufficient funds.

If battling dirt and disease were not exhausting enough, doctors also had many important administrative duties. They were responsible for testing the water, inspecting the kitchen, adjusting the diet and verifying the cleanliness of the dormitories. By law they had to be present at the infliction of any corporal punishment — and they had the authority to stop it if the prisoner's health was endangered.

In their spare time, they served on committees, kept accounts, compiled statistics, and prepared reports and recommendations for the inspectors. One surgeon was even asked to come up with a better method of brewing coffee.

Some penitentiary doctors were genuinely sympathetic toward their patients and championed their interest. Kingston Penitentiary's first physician, Dr. James Sampson, was a star witness against the Warden at the Brown Commission hearings in 1848.

Some, however, were lazy, corrupt and irresponsible. A surgeon at St. Vincent de Paul in the early 1900s was censured for lavishly dispensing narcotics to inmates.

Most doctors were not so indulgent. They usually erred on the side of severity and prided themselves on catching malingerers. Some of their suspicions were justified. Prisoners, then as now, reported imaginary illnesses and faked symptoms so they could enjoy the relatively easy life of the infirmary.

Nevertheless, there were many who were genuinely ill. During the period 1885-1935, many of the people admitted to penitentiaries were in very poor shape. In 1926, twenty five percent of incoming inmates were judged unfit for ordinary labour — they needed immediate medical attention. One prisoner received at Kingston in 1927 was simultaneously suffering from tuberculosis, venereal disease and scabies. The wretch was also a morphine addict.

Despite hard labour, coarse food and primitive hygiene standards, many inmates actually recovered their health in prison. In the 1920s, penitentiary records show that eighty percent of those discharged were in better physical condition and weighed more than when they had arrived.

In the 1930s, medical care in the penitentiaries was still substandard, but there were signs of improvement. Operating rooms and dental offices were opened, and prisoners benefited from recent medical discoveries. Prison doctors were more successful in controlling infectious diseases, but they noted with alarm the increase in social pathologies, such as drug abuse.

MILITARY PRISONERS

During its early years the penitentiary also admitted military prisoners. Kingston had been a military and naval centre since the War of 1812. Its strategic location at the junction of great lake and mighty river, with the newly independent United States on the opposite shore, dictated the building of the Rideau Canal by Colonel John By's engineers and sappers, a work that was completed in 1832. The canal was a marvel of construction for the world of the time. It was built to move supplies and troops quickly from Montréal to Kingston in the event of renewed hostilities with the U.S. It was a circuitous route, via the Ottawa River to Bytown (Ottawa) and through the Rideau waterway. But the straighter course along the St. Lawrence was blocked by the rapids at Lachine, the same rapids that stopped Jacques Cartier four hundred years before.

The perceived threat of incursion from the U.S. soon passed, but the Rideau Canal was an early measure of the importance of Kingston to the military. The tradition has continued in various ways, not least at the Royal Military College for officer cadets in the Canadian Armed

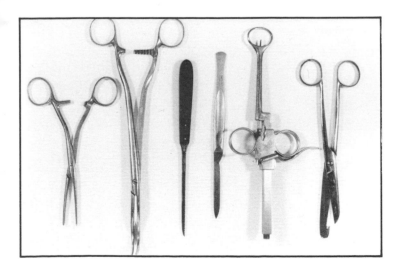

Forces. At Kingston Penitentiary, the presence of the military establishment has always been welcomed as back-up security in the event of a prison disturbance. The troops have marched through the North Gate more than once, as we shall see.

But in 1843, the soldiers were giving Warden Smith some headaches. The number of military prisoners had increased so significantly that he asked that their sentencing orders be changed to allow them to be put to hard labour, like the rest of the prison population. Warden Smith noted: "During the past year a number of convicts have

been committed to the Penitentiary for military offences, by the sentences of Court Martials, for periods varying from thirty days to two years; in some of the cases a part of the judgement of the Court was that a certain and specified portion of the period should be spent by the convict in solitary confinement and consequently without labour."

Warden Smith regarded the exclusion of military prisoners from hard labour as failing to carry out his mandate to provide strict discipline through work. As well, the military prisoners were regarded with envy by the general population of convicts who worked hard at cutting stone. The soldier prisoners were viewed as a privileged class, enjoying the relative peace and luxury of close confinement.

From the beginning, there was a close connection between the military and the penitentiary. In a letter to the Board of Inspectors dated October 1, 1838, Warden Smith noted: "the disturbed state of the country during the last winter having required increased watchfulness for the protection of the Penitentiary, every precaution was taken to put the establishment in as fit state of defence as the means placed at my disposal would admit." Smith was referring to the brief political insurrections of 1837. The extra guards placed on night duty became expensive because of the distance from Fort Henry (a few miles along Lake Ontario, but this could be hours away in an emergency, depending on weather and time). It was determined that a military guard would be garrisoned in the area. To that end, " a Guard-house and Barracks sufficient for the accommodation of forty men, have recently been erected on the Penitentiary grounds by the direction of the Commander of the Forces." For a short time the guard house and barracks were directly across from the North Gate, the main entrance to the penitentiary, on grounds later occupied by the Warden's residence.

THE GOVERNOR GENERAL'S RESIDENCE

The military presence was encouraged by the proximity of the Governor General of Canada. Three Governors General resided only a snowball's throw from the penitentiary at Alwington House, which stood on the lot of land immediately adjacent to Kingston Penitentiary on the east. Alwington was destroyed by fire in 1958 but for a dazzling three years a century before, it had been the focal point of political power and social success in pioneer Canada. When Kingston was picked as the capital of the united provinces of Upper and Lower Canada in 1841, Alwington was refurbished and enlarged at public expense and leased to the government to provide a dwelling for the Governor General, Lord Sydenham, and offices for his staff.

Unfortunately, Lord Sydenham did not enjoy the amenities for long. Less than four months after his arrival, he died at Alwington as the result of injuries sustained in a fall from his horse on King Street. In 1843 his successor, Sir Charles Bagot, also passed away there, within sight of the penitentiary's walls, which were still rising. The north towers would not be completed for another two years.

Sir Charles Metcalfe lived a year at Alwington before moving the capital and Government House to Montréal. This was in June 1844. Kingston Penitentiary was nine years old and already had cast its shadow over the start of a united Canada. It held three hundred and eighty four convicts in its cells. Before he departed, Governor General Metcalfe donated the first collection of non-religious books to the penitentiary, providing the nucleus of a prison

library. It would be another quarter century (1869) before "good conduct" prisoners would be permitted light in their cells to read by.

SOLDIERS WERE A CLASS ABOVE THE CRIMINALS

Warden Smith was finally successful in having the sentencing orders of the military prisoners altered, permitting him to use them at hard labour. In addition, some faced punishment of a more severe nature. Under the Mutiny Act, desertion was viewed as the most grievous offence possible. For this reason, deserters could be marked by tattoo with the letter "D".

With or without hard labour the Warden, who was very conscious of the need to defray costs, welcomed the presence of soldier convicts.

On their release from the penitentiary, military prisoners were required to surrender a portion of the pay they would have received as soldiers. This money was provided to the Warden as part of his subsistence. In his Annual Report for 1844-45, Warden Smith notes there were a hundred and fifteen soldiers at the penitentiary. They accounted for most of the increase in the population that year. By 1846, there were more than two hundred military prisoners. This arrangement would last for over twenty five years.

With the growth of the non-military prison population and the creation by the military of its own confinement, the use of the penitentiary for soldiers gradually withered away. It was increasingly opposed by the public as well. In 1848, the British Whig remarked on "the impropriety of sending soldiers to the penitentiary at Kingston for breaches of discipline . . . when a soldier loses his self-esteem, he is a lost man . . . one hour's confinement among the murderers and thieves of the penitentiary is enough to degrade a man in his own eyes forever." Soldiers, even errant ones, were of a class above the criminal.

But over the years circumstances would still conspire to bring the occasional soldier to Kingston Penitentiary. On June 26, 1951, more than a century later, inmate 1860 Doyle was "taken into Military Custody" and held for twelve days. During this period he was counted and held separately from the population of nine hundred and thirty three civilians who were there at the time.

1835 1985

CHAPTER III

YEARS OF CONTROVERSY

YEARS OF CONTROVERSY

Charles Dickens visited Kingston in 1842. Perhaps he was attracted here by the coincidence that Kingston, England, a penny ferry ride from Portsmouth, was the diocese of St. Mary's Church where he had been baptized. More likely he came on his American tour because he wanted to write about Canada for the readers back home, and Kingston happened to be the capital. It would not be for long, as Ontario and Québec contended for the political edge, moving the capital several times, from Kingston to Montréal to Toronto to Québec City, until Queen Victoria finally put a stop to it in 1857 by selecting Ottawa.

But he liked what he saw of the penitentiary. Dickens had a passion for prisons and described them well. He had reason to know, for his father had been imprisoned for debt in 1836, just six years earlier. Young Charles had been to an English prison daily for a few months to visit and bring bread for his dad. In his **American Notes**, he writes of Kingston Penitentiary, "There is an admirable gaol here, well and wisely governed, and excellently regulated, in every respect. The men were employed as shoemakers, ropemakers, blacksmiths, tailors, carpenters, and stonecutters; and in building a new prison, which was pretty far advanced toward completion. The female prisoners were occupied in needlework."

"WELL AND WISELY GOVERNED"

The great Victorian writer was not much taken by Kingston. He dismissed it in five sentences, summing it up as "a very poor town, rendered still poorer in the appearance of its market-place by the ravages of a recent fire (1840). Indeed, it may be said of Kingston, that one half of it appears to be burnt down, and the other half not to be built up."

Dickens observed an orderly, stable institution, the product of great bursts of activity and construction since its opening, spawned by the growing demand for cells and the need to complete the buildings so convicts could be turned to remunerative work. Indeed, Warden Smith had succeeded in getting the penitentiary on a well established footing.

A "BLACK PLAN" TO MOVE THE PENITENTIARY

Smith had already seen a number of controversies, not least a proposal by leading local tradesmen — mechanics as they were called — to move the penitentiary lock, stock and barriers to Marmora in the northwest, about sixty miles from Kingston. An iron works there could use the muscle from Kingston Penitentiary.

The issue had been simmering ever since the plan to build the penitentiary was announced. In

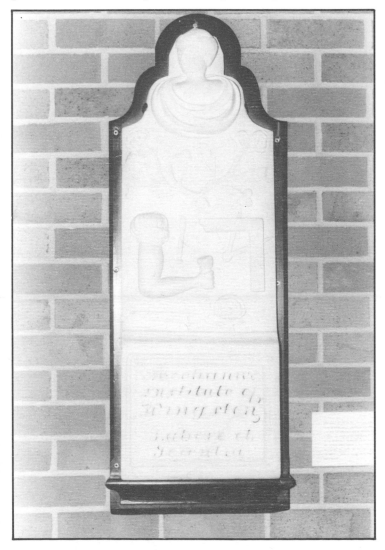

December 1833, an anonymous writer who described himself as "A Tradesman" protested the idea, claiming that it would take away trade from the local mechanics. "It is a black plan," he wrote. In an editorial accompanying this letter, the Chronicle retorted that over time the penitentiary would pay for itself and present no continuing burden to the taxpayer. This argument did little to reduce the outcry against the penitentiary from the newly formed Mechanic's Institute.

In February 1835, even before the arrival of any convicts, a public meeting in Kingston passed a resolution outlining the trades that the penitentiary should avoid at all costs. It also listed other trades that, while not prevalent in the area, should be avoided so that new mechanics would not be discouraged from entering into such trade in the future. It concluded that the only viable alternative was for the penitentiary to move to Marmora to operate the iron works. The resolution was moved by Mr. Oliver Mowat, uncle of the man who within a year would be articling at law in the office of Kingston barrister John A. Macdonald, and who later would become Premier of Ontario. It would not be the last time that debate about Kingston Penitentiary would colour the political landscape in Canada, and the careers of Canadian politicians. John A. Macdonald, who would always be a step ahead of pupil Mowat and became Canada's first Prime Minister, was closer to Kingston Penitentiary than to his downtown office when he lived at Bellevue House, now a national museum. He also owned the farmlot just behind the penitentiary property. John A. would get to know the prison well.

In his 1837 Annual Report, Warden Smith noted: "it has been throughout the object of the Inspectors to avoid any unnecessary interference

workforce could amount to hundreds of men. The prison was supposed to pay for itself out of the proceeds of their hard labour. It was threatening competition to some, and a remarkable opportunity to others. Four years after the Mowat resolution, a report to the Upper Canada House of Assembly in 1839 recommended the removal of the penitentiary to occupy the grounds and reopen the Marmora Iron Works, which had fallen into disuse. The recommendation was made over the objection of the chairman of the reporting commission, Mr. Peter McGill, who

with the interests of Mechanics by prohibiting the manufacturing for sale of such articles as were likely to injure the business of individual tradesmen." With those words, he was to articulate one of the fundamental dilemmas of penitentiaries: the need to provide employment for the occupation and training of inmates and to pay for the operating costs of the penitentiary while avoiding competition with private industry.

The issue would not go away. There were commercial interests at stake. The prison

disagreed with the concept of removal because of its cost. In his view, the expenditures already made at Portsmouth would be completely lost. Nor were there very many creative suggestions about what might be done with the penitentiary buildings if the prisoners went elsewhere. It was not as if they could be converted easily to other uses. They certainly could not be knocked down. The walls were of limestone. They were three feet thick.

From within the penitentiary, the most articulate defence of the Portsmouth site was given by Deputy Warden Powers. He confronted the issue of convict labour with an argument which has relevance even to this day: "What ever objections may be made against productive mechanical labour in a penitentiary, will apply with equal force and reason against water and steam power, and against all inventions and improvements in the labour saving machinery; which improvements, by facilitating manufacturing operations, and increasing the product of individual labour, thirty, fifty or perhaps a hundred fold, notwithstanding its dense population, has made England rich." Powers confronted the mechanics on their own ground, suggesting that all imported goods should be subject to the same strictures, concluding that "if the reformation of wretched convicts of the Penitentiary, and their return to honest industry, are an injury to the interests of the Mechanics, then are their interests directly opposed to the best interests of society, the principles of Christian benevolence, and the human object of the Government."

The penitentiary did not move to Marmora, although the iron works did reopen and prospered without convict labour. Nonetheless, the issue served to alert those within the penitentiary community of the need to move cautiously in what was already a sensitive area and was destined to remain so.

CONFLICT WITHIN

Warden Smith was not an easy man to work with. He could be obstinate and even vengeful. The first object of his ire was his own Deputy, William Powers, the American whose experience had made the rapid building of the penitentiary possible. By the late 1830s Smith and Powers were no longer on speaking terms. Controversy between them continued until Powers felt compelled to resign. There was no reluctance by staff and citizens to see this conflict discussed publicly, often in lengthy, anonymous letters to local and Toronto papers. In retrospect the real issue seems to have been Warden Smith's desire or drive to dominate Kingston Penitentiary in every way.

In the early 1840s, Smith's will prevailed. However, for reasons that are not entirely clear, he became less and less involved in the daily operation of the penitentiary. Though he had the power he needed, he was excessively jealous of any authority wielded by subordinates. Smith's capacity for revenge and intrigue reached their height in his treatment of Edward Utting, who eventually succeeded Powers as deputy, and Dr. Sampson, the penitentiary surgeon. With the help of his son, who was a Conservative member of the House of Assembly, Smith virtually rewrote the Penitentiary Act in 1846 to reduce the salaries of all senior penitentiary officials with one important exception, himself. His remuneration was increased thereby inflaming his opponents all the more. Their differences appear to have been sparked less by matters of substance than by passionate personality conflicts.

By 1847, matters had reached a crisis. Various senior staff members were pitted against Smith, in public. They were supported by the leading opposition newspapers. The election of a new Reform government that year reduced Smith's political leverage. A commission was appointed to investigate the conduct, discipline and management at the Provincial Penitentiary. Its chairman was the Honourable Adam Ferguson. But the proceedings were to be dominated by its secretary, George Brown.

George Brown was editor of the Toronto Globe and would soon be elected a Reform member of the legislature. His newspaper survives as The Globe and Mail, by common consent the most prominent daily newspaper in Anglophone Canada. His name resounds in Canadian history as the lifelong rival and most worthy antagonist of John A. Macdonald throughout their long, entangled political careers. Their rivalry had its origins early along their paths to greatness, when they squared off in Kingston. There was no doubt that Brown, the Reformer from Toronto, was going to scalp the Warden. John A. was the sitting Tory member for Kingston and a friend of the Smith family. Then as now, the penitentiary had explosive political potential. A clash was inevitable.

THE FIRST PUBLIC INQUIRY

The "Brown Report" issued in May, 1849, was a scathing attack on Henry Smith's administration of Kingston Penitentiary, as even then it was known throughout British North America. It painted a picture of a harsh, brutal, dehumanizing régime in which corporal punishment was meted out fiercely, repeatedly and indiscriminately, usually at the order of Warden

Smith. He would not administer the beatings himself. That was not the way, then or later.

Corporal punishment, though much reduced in frequency, continued at Kingston Penitentiary for more than a century after the Smith régime. It was not formally abolished until 1972. Officers still serving can remember the drill on punishment parade. The inmate was brought in to the Keeper's Hall, stripped and buckled to the bench at his ankles, waist and wrists. The strapping table was a modification of the examining table in a doctor's office. The inmate lay face down, fitted with dark goggles to prevent him from identifying the officer giving the beating. There would be several officers present. The Warden, his deputy or the chief keeper would hand the strap to any one of them, usually without forewarning, and he was to step forward smartly to administer the strokes. He was not to stroke lightly. The doctor, who by law had to be there, could put a stop to it if the toll on the body threatened permanent injury.

The commissioners were severely critical of the practice of corporal punishment, particularly as it was applied to child convicts. They reported the case of convict Peter Charbonneau, a ten-

year-old serving seven years. The punishment book noted that Charbonneau's prison offences were of a trifling nature, like staring, winking and laughing—behaviour one would expect of a young boy. But for this he was stripped of his shirt and publicly lashed fifty seven times in eight and a half months.

There was also the case of Antoine Beauche, sentenced to three years in November, 1845. The report notes that this eight-year-old received the lash within a week of his arrival and was given no

fewer than forty seven lashings in nine months. A French-Canadian boy, Alec Lafleur, aged eleven years, was given the lash on Christmas Eve, 1844, for speaking French.

Women convicts were not spared similar treatment. One fourteen-year-old, Sarah O'Connor, was flogged on five occasions during a three-month period. Another, Elizabeth Breen, aged twelve, was flogged five times in four months. The report went on to cite numerous instances of cruel and barbaric practice such as this and concluded that "the practice of flogging women is utterly indefensible."

Frank Smith was the Warden's son. He was certainly not as distinguished as his brother, Henry Smith Jr., the Tory member for Frontenac, who later would be named Speaker of the Assembly and become Sir Henry at the touch of the Prince of Wales during his 1860 Canadian visit. It was a visit which touched Kingston and Kingston Penitentiary as well (see Chapter V).

Frank Smith was employed as a keeper in the kitchen. He was named as one of the ringleaders in the reign of brutality that the Brown Commission discovered and thoroughly documented. Frank Smith was charged by the penitentiary surgeon, James Sampson, with shooting arrows at convicts for target practice, blinding one inmate, throwing inmates into water barrels, ordering them to open their mouths and then spitting into them, selling government shoes, using convict labour for his own benefit and assaulting women convicts.

The Brown Report resulted in Warden Smith's immediate resignation, and the dismissal of son Frank, along with other prison officers.

It was the first of many brooms that would sweep through the penal system over the years. From this one penitentiary on the outskirts of Kingston with about a hundred and fifty cells, the nationwide system would grow to more than sixty federal penitentiaries holding a population of more than eleven thousand criminals. They were called convicts until 1914 and prisoners until 1939. Currently they are more often referred to as inmates. Similarly, watchmen became guards, and are known now as correctional officers (CX in Service shorthand). Keepers are still keepers. They lead the daily security operation. Wardens are still wardens.

HARD TIMES

Warden Smith was one of a kind and his record of savage repression has never since been approached. But it is only fair to point out that he came first to a new post of authority in a young nation. He was given strict instructions by the legislators, none of whom knew any more about penitentiaries than the average pioneer politician, and he interpreted them strictly. Any other course, in his view, would have been a dereliction of duty. Even as it was, at the height of the Brown revelations, the British Colonist could editorialize that, "The march of refined benevolence has converted our prisons into palaces." This was an outcome devoutly to be avoided, in the opinion of the leaders of the day. William Lyon Mackenzie wrote on the subject as Kingston Penitentiary was being built, arguing that a prison sentence must not become preferable to a criminal's ordinary lifestyle. The penitentiary had to be truly inhospitable. Hardship was to be institutionalized.

Moreover, the times themselves were very hard, even in the free society. Sometimes harvests were good, but frequently enough they failed. There were hungry years in Canada in the first half of the nineteenth century. The winters could be harsh. There was a great flood of migrants, some of whom would get to know the inside of Kingston Penitentiary. For many years a strict record was kept of the national origin of the population. "Unprepared and badly equipped to meet the loneliness, the poverty, the incessant, brutalizing toil of the backwoods," writes historian Donald Creighton, "they often escaped complete shipwreck only by sacrifices in health and education which impoverished their cultural life and degraded their standards of living." For most people, daily life was full of discomforts and un-

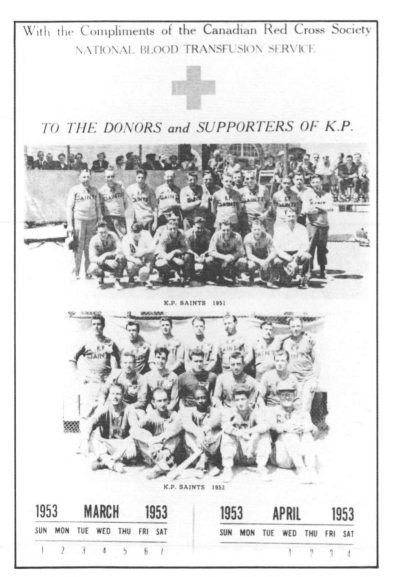

With the Compliments of the Canadian Red Cross Society
NATIONAL BLOOD TRANSFUSION SERVICE

TO THE DONORS and SUPPORTERS OF K.P.

K.P. SAINTS 1951

K.P. SAINTS 1952

1953	MARCH				1953		1953	APRIL				1953
SUN	MON	TUE	WED	THU	FRI	SAT	SUN	MON	TUE	WED	THU	FRI	SAT
	1	2	3	4	5	6	7				1	2	3	4

certainties. Poverty was the rule, hard work the only hope. It was not a society that wanted its criminals coddled.

THE WARDEN'S POWERS ARE REDUCED

John A. Macdonald presented a petition on behalf of Smith. It was voted down by the government members. The future father of confederation was thirty five years old. He would not be-come Attorney General of Canada West for another four years, at which time he would find the penitentiary in his portfolio as well as in his riding. His defence of Smith was based on friendship for the Warden and his son Henry Jr. more than any conviction that an injustice was being done. In the end it gained nothing for Smith, but it fuelled the feud with George Brown, erupting in debate in the legislature as late as 1856. It also gave Macdonald the opportunity to acquaint himself with conditions at Kingston Penitentiary. He would be there frequently in years to come, on official visits, in the company of other dignitaries. He came to some conclusions about penitentiaries and prisoners, which he would share with his friend John Creighton when he was named Warden.

After the Brown Commission reported, legislative changes were made which reduced the power and authority of the Warden. Responsibility for the hiring and firing of staff was vested in the Board of Inspectors, which for a brief time had George Brown as one of its members. This régime was to continue until more penitentiaries were built across the country in the 1870s.

The period between the admission of the first six inmates to Kingston Penitentiary and publication of the Brown Report was a time of continuous change, even turmoil. Warden Smith was confronted by many challenges and conflicting goals. He had to open the penitentiary with inadequate funding from the House of Assembly. As soon as possible, he was to create self-sustaining industry so that returns from the use of convict labour would recoup the cost of building and maintaining the penitentiary. He also had to avoid the dangerous issue of competition with the local mechanics. It was not a winning hand for anyone to be dealt. Kingston's first Warden, though, played it about as badly as anyone could. He was his own worst enemy, constantly engaged in monumental dispute with all around him. His antagonists included colleagues on whom he had to depend for the security of the institution, the public, the politicians and, most unfortunately for them, the prisoners.

PROVINCIAL PENITENTIARY.

RETURN

To an Address from the Legislative Assembly to His Excellency the Governor General, dated the 30th instant, praying that His Excellency would be pleased to cause to be laid before them, "a Copy of the Reports made by the Commissioners " appointed to investigate into the Conduct, Discipline, and Management of the Pro- " vincial Penitentiary, with the Documents transmitted by the Commissioners."

By Command,

J. LESLIE,
Secretary.

Provincial Secretary's Office,
Montreal, 30th May, 1849.

Provincial Penitentiary Commission Room,
Montreal, 20th March, 1849.

Sir,

I have the honour to transmit herewith the First Report of the Penitentiary Commission.

The Second and Final Report of the Commission will be submitted to His Excellency with the least possible delay.

I have the honour to be,
Sir,
Your most obedient Servant,

GEO. BROWN,
Secretary.

Honourable James Leslie,
Provincial Secretary.

Secretary's Office,
22nd March, 1849.

Sir,

I have had the honour to receive and lay before His Excellency the Governor General, the First Report of the Penitentiary Commission, which was transmitted with your letter of the 20th instant.

I have, &c.,

JAS. LESLIE.

Geo. Brown, Esquire,
Secretary,
Penitentiary Commission.

CHAPTER IV

WINDS OF CHANGE

WINDS OF CHANGE

Following George Brown's scandalous revelations and the departure of Warden Smith, Donald Aeneas MacDonell was appointed Warden of Kingston Penitentiary. Under his guidance, the penitentiary entered a period of stability and relative quiet. Like his predecessor, Warden MacDonell was a disciplinarian fully commited to the Auburn silent system. The extent to which his charges would go to circumvent these harsh regulations is graphically illustrated in this excerpt from his Warden's Journal:

"I visited the prison between 8 and 9 o'clock. All there reported quiet. While I was visiting the East Wing, one of the convicts in the First North broke wind in a very brutal manner. This is one of the ways which these unfortunate beings take to give annoyance but such acts only show the brutality of the parties and what they would do if not deterred by fear."

THE WARDEN'S ROUTINE

The Warden's workday began at about 5 a.m., when he delivered the penitentiary keys to the guard on duty. The bell would be rung and the Chaplain would say the morning prayers. Warden MacDonell would watch the prisoners pass from their cells, with their buckets to be dumped, and proceed to breakfast. Convicts would have arrived at their workplaces by 7:15. After his own breakfast, the Warden would attend to general office business, visit various shops, the hospital and the women's prison. He would attend to the Punishment Book and receive visitors before observing the prisoner's lunch hour. In the afternoon he would visit workgangs and deal with staff and prisoner discipline problems. He would be at dinner with the population at 6 p.m., and afterwards might read a letter to a convict. His day was not done until he was confident that the institution was "all thru' quiet."

The Warden's official duties and responsibilities were awesome. He was directly involved in all aspects of prison life. He dealt with the food and clothing of all convicts and prison officials, health, security, business negotiations with Canadian and American contractors, purchases of goods, hiring and firing, punishment of prisoners, recording of deaths within the walls, collection of money owed to the prison, release of prisoners as ordered by the Governor General, and correspondence with families or others concerned about inmates inside the penitentiary. He was a powerful figure, but his authority was not unfettered. He reported directly to the Inspectors, who routinely investigated matters at the penitentiary. They had to be informed not only about unusual events, such as unexpected escapes, deaths or murders, but also such regular matters as releases, internal staff disputes, contractual negotiations and petitions for higher salaries or sick pay. Perhaps the greatest constraint he faced was the tight control by the Governor General's office of the funds allocated for the general purposes of the institution. A great deal of the Warden's correspondence is taken up with applications for more money, and follow-up when it is not forthcoming.

CONTINUED EMPHASIS ON PUNISHMENT

Warden MacDonell's first annual report was issued in 1850. The reduction in the number of punishments was a matter of some pride: for the population of about four hundred prisoners, just 2,782 punishments. This was less than half the number meted out three years before, under Smith. And while the Warden wrote that he was "still of the opinion, that the punishment of the Cats cannot be dispensed with," in fact he inflicted this fearsome sentence only five times in the year. For the most part, his punishments were for bread and water diets, usually lasting three meals or less.

But such leniency was not fated to last. By 1859 the population had swelled to more than nine hundred and the total number of punishments for the year exceeded 9,000. The great majority were still bread and water sentences, or confinement in a dark cell. But there were sixty cuts of the switch inflicted on nine junior convicts and six hundred and sixteen lashes of the cats for twenty seven adult prisoners. Twelve convicts were shackled in chains, although the Warden remarks that only two of these have worn the heavy iron for the full year, and "they are both desperate characters."

His views may have hardened even further. When his successor first reported in 1870, he wrote that he found "five convicts wearing a chain; one had carried it for six months, three for seven months, and one for nine years! In the last case, it had not even been taken off when the man was *sick* in hospital."

AN ASYLUM FOR THE "CRIMINAL LUNATICS"

It is quite conceivable that the convict so treated was insane. The problem of dealing with "criminal lunatics" was one that would plague all of the early wardens, and indeed the entire penitentiary system until the 1930s. The causes and treatment of mental illness were not understood. The practice in the early nineteenth century was to send disruptive lunatics to local gaols for "restraint" if they could not be cared for by their families at home. The more severe their disorder or violent their behaviour, the more likely it was they would commit crimes that would bring penitentiary sentences. The insane have difficulty with all rules, but particularly the rule of silence that was so sacrosanct at Kingston Penitentiary. They were beaten often enough, but they could not be silenced. They drove the prison routine to distraction and in retaliation the system mandated cruelties that drove them further into madness.

John Solomon Cartwright of Kingston was chairman of the first government commission to examine the need to house and treat the mentally ill in Upper Canada. His recommendation led to the first provincial asylum at 999 Queen St. W. in Toronto, built in the early 1840s. This was quickly filled. However, it had no facilities for those who were sentenced by the courts — criminal lunatics.

John Cartwright's home was called Rockwood. It stood on an estate just above Hatter's Bay, across the harbour from the new penitentiary. When Cartwright died near Christmas 1845, his widow offered Rockwood for rent at £60 a year. One of the early tenants was Dr. John Litchfield, who had held responsible medical posts in Australia and England, and was to be among the first medical lecturers at Queen's, an instructor "in the important subject of psychological medicine." He also took patients into his home for care. They tended to be "well-to-do gentlemen of unsound mind."

Here at Rockwood, across the bay from Kingston Penitentiary, Canada's first treatment centre for the criminally insane began to evolve.

In 1856 the government purchased thirty five acres of the Cartwright estate for £5,000. The first priority was to find a place for females, since Dr. Litchfield did not want them in his house mixing with males. The temporary solution was to fix up the stables on the property. Twenty secure rooms were built, with four strong cells, and rooms for the keepers and for dining. The rooms were nine feet by five feet, with a door two feet wide. A barred peephole, high in the wall, provided the only source of light and fresh air. Even so, it was thought to be elaborate for its purpose, according to this doggerel of the day, attributed to Kingston Penitentiary's first surgeon, James Sampson:

"Oh, would to God that I were able
To build a house like Cartwright's stable.
For it fills my heart with great remorse,
To be worse housed than Cartwright's horse."

The building of a permanent asylum started in 1859, halfway through the tenure of Warden MacDonell at Kingston Penitentiary. He would have an important role to play. Convict labour would be used to construct the buildings, under the direction of architect William Coverdale. The medical superintendent at Rockwood reported to

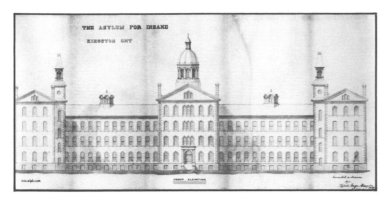

THE ASYLUM FOR INSANE
KINGSTON ONT

FRONT ELEVATION

the Kingston Penitentiary Warden until 1877, when Rockwood was taken over by the province of Ontario, and renamed. It is still in service, known as the Kingston Psychiatric Hospital, having been rebuilt and added to over the years. In its earliest days it was rushed to completion so that twenty one lunatics confined in the basement of the Kingston Penitentiary dining hall could be removed. Warden MacDonell wrote of Rockwood that its "speedy completion is imperiously called for . . . the increased space is loudly demanded . . . for the removal of the wretched creatures under the dining hall in this institution. These poor afflicted beings are not only debarred from out-door exercise, but are exceedingly cramped in their present location; also they are, to a great degree, deprived of the cheering and healthful influence of the sun and air; and, worse still, are pent up in a close, damp space, a very cellar, the exhalations emanating from which — let alone the other pernicious concomitants — are exceedingly detrimental to physical and mental health; and there can be no doubt but for the extreme care, good and enlightened treatment of these persons by Dr. Litchfield, the talented superintendent, that the suffering and mortality would be most grievous."

Rockwood was formally opened in 1865, although space had been made three years before to get the insane convicts out of the cellar at Kingston Penitentiary. It stood four storeys high on a frontage of three hundred and ten feet, "the entire building having been constructed by convicts alone, thus furnishing a very large building at a very small cost to the country." There was room for three hundred patients.

RESTORING STAFF DISCIPLINE

Warden MacDonell would be the longest-serving Warden in the history of Kingston Penitentiary. He would also be the last Warden of the provincial penitentiary and the first of Kingston Penitentiary, which it was formally named at the time of Confederation in 1867. On July 1 of that year, John A. Macdonald of Kingston was knighted and sworn in as the new Dominion's first Prime Minister. But Sir John A. did not allow the duties of his great office to deflect him from local concerns. The Cartwright family still lived on their estate, adjacent to the land they had sold for Rockwood. They wanted a fence between their home and the asylum. The new P.M. intervened himself, ordering an estimate of the cost of such a wall and offering the opinion that the family, which he knew well, "has a right to

insist upon such a wall being built and not to be liable to the intrusion of lunatics."

On May 10, 1869, James Ferres succeeded MacDonell as Warden. He was to die in office after only a year, but first he would right a number of wrongs that he felt had crept in under his predecessor's long tenure. Warden Smith's administration had been too severe and strict with the prisoners. Warden MacDonell's legacy was laxity and permissiveness among prison officers, at least in the view of Warden Ferres, who wrote in his first annual report that "officers have been permitted to come on duty under the influence of liquor, and more than one of them, high in rank in a state of daily intoxication (and) have been found delinquent in their conduct, in various degrees, even up to being asleep on their posts. . ."

Warden Ferres had previously been the Inspector of Penitentiaries, Jails and Asylums, and he knew whereof he spoke. He commented that the abuses had been going on for years "in disregard of the remonstrances of the Inspectors" and he was determined to restore discipline. He did not expect it to be easy.

"There will be no difficulty in understanding that, in an establishment in which over a hundred officers are employed, with such a disorganization prevailing, there would be many to whom a change to restraint, however moderate, would be distasteful and the author of the change regarded in the light of an oppressor; and the greater the license, which length of time had constituted the rule, the more bitter the repugnance to submit to wholesome discipline.

"Such are the feelings, with some exceptions, which I have found prevalent among all classes of officers."

EARLY PRIVILEGES FOR CONVICTS

While bearing down on staff, Warden Ferres started to ease up on some of the harsher aspects of convict life. He set apart the west wing for prisoners of "exemplary conduct", who were distinguished by having three stripes sewn to the sleeve of their uniforms. This wing was lighted at night until nine o'clock. These "men of the advanced class" were also allowed to walk for an hour in the prison yard on Sundays, and "as occasion justifies" might be allowed to write more than the one letter every three months which was the rule.

This element of earned privileges and recognition would play an ever greater role in the management of convicts as time progressed. An act had been passed in 1868 establishing federal institutions under the jurisdiction of the Minister of Justice and also providing, for the first time a program of earned remission of sentence for convicts, under which they might shorten their time in penitentiary by their own efforts. Warden Ferres saw the results immediately, writing in 1870: "It is highly gratifying to observe the excellent effect which the privilege, granted in the

Penitentiary Act, to a convict to earn a remittance of five days per month off his sentence, has had upon the prisoners . . . this remission is a powerful means of inducing industry and good behaviour." Of the two hundred and forty one prisoners discharged that year, two hundred and twenty four had earned at least some remission.

Education was another privilege, which prisoners had enjoyed in very small doses since the first teacher was hired in 1852. Warden Ferres believed that the state "is entitled to the full day's labour of every man who is sent here for punishment, and that the teaching he is to receive in the common branches of education should be given him . . . after the hours of labour." Even so, he extended instruction from one-and-a-half hours a week in the cells to fourteen hours in a classroom.

The emphasis on education was not entirely for the purposes of improving the minds of convict students. It was seen also as a reason to let them out of their cells, which were cramped beyond endurance. The Warden acknowledged that "the convicts in this prison are too long pent up in their cells. In the width of them, there is not one inch more than the width of their bed, and in the length only about a couple of feet free to spare. To be enclosed in so contracted a space for nearly twelve hours during the summer months, and for over twelve hours during the winter, is bad for the convicts physically and bad for them morally."

He refers to a report on colonial prisons prepared by the British government, which "emphatically objects" to prisoners lying too long in bed. "This Penitentiary," he writes, "is especially faulty in this respect — because the convict, when locked up, has no choice but to lie down, seeing there is no space for him in which to move." The cells were not going to get any larger until the turn of the century, and then not much

larger. They are still not spacious, although inmates in 1985 have access to a common area along the wide range that runs between their barred doors and the exterior wall of the cell block. In the evening, until the final count at eleven, officers walk the ranges every hour, letting inmates out of their cells, or locking them back in, on request.

MORE PENITENTIARIES CONSTRUCTED

The first years of the new Dominion brought great changes to all the institutions of nationhood, not least Canada's penitentiaries. It was a time for prison construction, first St. Vincent de Paul in 1873, Stony Mountain in Manitoba in 1877, British Columbia Penitentiary in 1878 (closed in 1980) and Dorchester in New Brunswick in 1880. All the new institutions were learning their lessons and taking their lead from Kingston Penitentiary, the original and still the toughest pen in the country. For the first five years St. Vincent de Paul sent its hardest cases on to Kingston, and when this practice stopped they discovered that it made a difference. The report of the Minister of Justice on penitentiaries for 1880

sent for training to Kingston Penitentiary, and later to the Correctional Service of Canada induction centre and staff college which were located in Kingston. During the twentieth century, the city would become the corrections centre of Canada, with eight federal penitentiaries within a fifteen mile radius, as well as the staff colleges with their modern, computer-assisted training programs. Kingston became, and still is, the Ontario regional headquarters for the Correctional Service.

RENEWED EMPHASIS ON REFORM

The 1870s also began an era of prison reform. In 1871, John Creighton was appointed the fourth Warden of the penitentiary, a post he held until his death in 1885. Warden Creighton's reasonable disposition and concern for the welfare of the inmates worked very well to maintain the good order which Kingston Penitentiary enjoyed during his tenure. Like Smith and MacDonell, Warden Creighton was a political appointee. A close friend and former schoolmate of Prime Minister Macdonald, he had been Mayor of Kingston and a police magistrate. He came to the penitentiary with an

makes the point that "since we have discontinued sending to Kingston our most unmanageable prisoners, it is becoming harder to keep up the same discipline as formerly. In certain connections these migrations, which took place once or twice in each year, were of great assistance to us, in that they enabled us to free ourselves of the most difficult cases to deal with."

Officers from Kingston would frequently be sent out to take command or train staff at the newer institutions. Keepers and other staff were outstanding civic career behind him as preparation for the task.

John Creighton was intent upon reform. His zeal was both encouraged and tempered by his mentor, Sir John A. The Prime Minister wrote to Warden Creighton, "Your ultimate success in making the Penitentiary a school of reform, as well as a place of punishment is worthwhile, but my only fear is that your natural kindness of disposition may lead you to forget that the primary purpose of the penitentiary is punishment and the incidental one reformation. There is such a thing as making a prison too comfortable and prisoners too happy."

Warden Creighton's first annual report in 1871 mentions some of the changes that were ameliorating the hard life inside. Coal oil lighting was introduced into the cells of preferred inmates. Three months of good conduct might be rewarded with light in one's cell until nine o'clock. The new system of remission for inmates, which also entitled them to a gratuity on their release, was extensively and generously applied. The Warden was ruled by compassion and the impulse

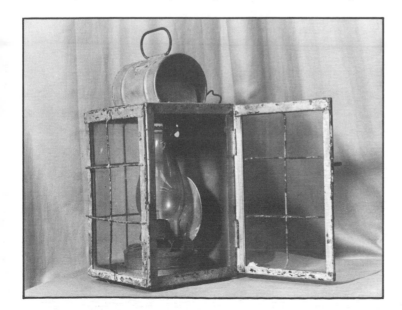

to be fair in his dealings with all his charges, offenders as well as officers. More than any other pioneer of the penitentiary service, he embodied fairness — that instinct which is most highly regarded in a correctional officer. To be fair is not always easy when provoked or assaulted or deceived, abuses which prison officers must endure as part of their job. But to manage any group of human beings, even criminals, requires fair treatment if there is to be hope of success without resorting to force and repression.

The spirit of change was most evident in Creighton's approach to discipline. In his report of 1872 he notes that his "milder" course had led to an end of the lash. Throughout his tenure Warden Creighton repeatedly expresses loathing for corporal punishment. However he saw and used solitary confinement as an alternative.

His milder approach did not render Warden Creighton any more immune to the perils faced by everyone who works with inmates, then and now. On May 15, 1876, he was attacked and stabbed in the convict dining room. The incident was reported in the British Whig:

"REFRACTORY CONVICT - Yesterday a convict named Blake exhibited his ugly temper in the Kingston Penitentiary by a villainous assault upon the Warden during breakfast hour. It seems that the prisoner had risen from his place contrary to rule, and refused to seat himself when directed to do so by Mr. Creighton, who was present. The latter saw the necessity of having his orders obeyed, and catching the convict gently by the arm attempted to force him to comply when he stabbed the Warden in the groin with a three-tined fork which he held in his hand. The wound, we are glad to learn, is not of serious import. Any convict who can be so vicious under Mr. Creighton's management of affairs deserves no leniency, but the severest penalty that can be imposed. Kindness is shown to all convicts, and if punishment is meted out occasionally, it is because the cases are such that it cannot be avoided."

By his own account, Warden Creighton was not badly hurt and he returned to work the same day. Despite the Whig's allusion there is no evidence that the inmate was punished for his intemperate attack. Perhaps the Warden was reluctant to send him to isolation in the dungeon, mindful of the fact that convict Maurice Blake had been there before, and had witnessed one of the most incredible feats ever accomplished in Kingston Penitentiary, an escape from the hole. It had happened the year before, in 1875, and convict Blake would take another crack a few years later before the dungeon was finally sealed (see Chapter IX).

Warden Creighton's stewardship at Kingston Penitentiary set the stage for other periods of growth and change affecting the treatment of convicts, reform movements which continue to the present day as each generation of Canadians redefines the way it wants to treat criminals. There is no doubt that whatever good is accomplished in today's penitentiaries owes a substantial debt to the example and the work of John Creighton, a pioneer of the Canadian public service.

CHAPTER V

HARD LABOUR

HARD LABOUR

For many years, work in the penitentiary meant hard labour. Five of the original six inmates who arrived in 1835 were immediately placed under the direction of a keeper to learn stonecutting. This trade was to continue at the prison for over one hundred years. The sixth was the cook.

The philosophy of work in Kingston Penitentiary was twofold. It was intended to make the penitentiary self-sustaining and also to assist in reforming the convict. The work ethic was strongly ingrained in the character of the day's business, moral and political leaders, who were the citizens most likely to know anything about who was in Kingston Penitentiary and what went on there.

LEASED LABOUR

During the first fifteen years (1835-1850) most of the convict labour was used in building and maintaining the penitentiary. The convicts worked six days a week, from dawn until dusk. By

1848, most of the penitentiary buildings, walls and towers were completed. The Board of Inspectors then began leasing the labour of the convicts by contract to private entrepreneurs who were prepared to set up their production lines within the walls. This practice was introduced by a government intent upon making the penitentiary self-supporting.

In 1849 the labour of two hundred convicts was let to Messrs. E.P. Ross as shoemakers, Stevenson of Napanee as cabinetmakers, Brown as tailors and Stevenson as blacksmiths. All of these contracts were for a five year period, at a rate of one shilling and six pence, about 30 cents, per day per convict. Twenty years later the rate had improved to 40 cents per day.

The prisoners did not receive any direct benefit from this remuneration, since all revenues generated by convict labour were used to defray the costs of their incarceration.

In 1853, the Board of Inspectors indicated that their contract with Mr. Ross was "not entirely satisfactory." They had discovered that he was paying for convict labour only half what he was paying for the same work at Auburn Prison in New York. Notwithstanding this and other disagreements between contractors and penitentiary authorities, the contract system was to flourish at Kingston Penitentiary for many years.

Some local businessmen in fact owed their prosperity to the availability of a guaranteed supply of convict labour. The practice provided revenues to the penitentiary, and sometimes a trade for inmates, an important element in their hope to maintain themselves in free society on release. J.P. Millner and Company of Kingston advertised in these terms in 1857:

"Having taken the management of the Blacksmith Shop in the Provincial Penitentiary and secured the service of the best Mechanics as foremen, we are confident we can turn out as good an article, and at a cheaper rate than any manufacturer in Canada."

PRODUCTS OF VALUE AND VARIETY

The products of some shops were displayed in the store windows of the city's merchants. The public could hardly fail to see the value and variety of the articles manufactured in the penitentiary, which were also on display at the popular merchandising fairs of the day, including many held at the Crystal Palace in mid-century.

The Palace sat on a piece of land leased from the penitentiary at the north end of its lot, opposite John A. Macdonald's farm. The main prison products of the day on display would have been furniture, shoes, hay forks, and other light farm implements.

In 1860 the penitentiary entered into a contract with a local cabinetmaker, Samuel T. Drennan. The penitentiary supplied the buildings, provided the heating, guards, and convict labour for a furniture factory inside the prison walls. Drennan's retail outlet was situated on Princess Street in Kingston, in premises known as the Lambton Buildings. His plant was in Kingston Penitentiary.

In September 1860, Edward, Prince of Wales was scheduled to visit Kingston. In the Prince's honour, an impressive and ornately carved chair was crafted by convicts at the Drennan factory inside the walls. However, the local Orange Order, a militant Protestant organization, built an arch through which His Royal Highness would have to pass upon entering the city. Rather than risk a religious controversy, the Prince heeded advice not to disembark from the Royal yacht or set foot in the city. The celebrations were greatly upset, but some artifacts of the historic incident survived. In 1983, descendants of Mr. Drennan donated the convict-made chair to the city. It now occupies a place of honour in Memorial Hall at Kingston City Hall, where it is resplendent in public view under a portrait of the former cabinetmaker, who also served a term as Mayor of Kingston, His Worship Samuel Drennan.

In 1876, an order was received at the penitentiary for a large and varied assortment of furniture for the Royal Military College, which opened in Kingston later that year. The tailor and shoe shops were producing the scarlet tunics, grey breeches and high, brown boots that would identify the newly-created (1874) North West Mounted Police. But the convicts were not working solely on light goods. During the same period Kingston Penitentiary furnished cast and wrought iron for the Parliamentary Library in Ottawa. There was real industrial capability inside the closely-guarded perimeter. Canadian Pacific Railway was a customer. One order was for thirty "frogs" and switch frames, weighing thirty three tons, for railroad shunting. With one day's notice in October 1875, Warden Creighton had a gang ready at the penitentiary dock to

unload four barges of iron rails, weighing 1,225 tons, "to be stored for the Dominion Government." The penitentiary filled numerous orders from government agencies including the Federal Board of Public Works and other penitentiaries.

SECURITY VIGILANT AS WORK GOES ON

Overseeing this industrial hubbub were armed guards in the tall towers, manned twenty-four hours a day. Most prison guards did not carry guns, to minimize the possibility that they might be snatched by convicts. But there have always been a number of secure, strategic posts that contain weapons. Arms were among the first supplies ordered by Warden Smith, before the arrival of any convicts. By 1856, during the tenure of Warden MacDonell, the penitentiary had settled on "Colt's patent pistols" as sidearms for officers.

The five towers remain the final guarantee and symbol of security at Kingston Penitentiary, and tower guards are still armed. In 1985, as the hundred and fiftieth year of the institution passes, Tower One in the northeast corner is supplied

with a .38 revolver and a Colt AR-15 semi-automatic rifle, with ten slugs in the magazine and two spare clips. Each of the other four towers has the same.

Nineteenth century weapons were different, but the vigilance was constant, as it had to be. The officer's job was to keep the convicts in. Security never relaxed as the work went on, in the shops and in convict gangs, sometimes using every ray of daylight if there were heavy deadlines to meet. There were always conflicts between the objectives of tight security and the requirements of contractors who had orders to get out. It was a conflict eventually resolved, not for reasons of security, but because the penitentiary's industries were becoming too competitive with free enterprise. In 1883 penitentiary industries were formally prohibited from competing with private companies.

NEW CONSTRUCTION TO REDUCE IDLENESS

The contract system ended completely in 1886, much to the dismay of both the Warden and the contractors. The Warden was now forced to find or invent other ways to occupy the inmates, who were still sentenced to hard labour. The judges meant it, society expected it and it was up to the Warden to find work for hundreds of men with nothing but time on their hands and often resentment and anger in their hearts. The contractors saw their source of cheap labour dry up. Warden Michael Lavell, who succeeded Warden Creighton on February 3, 1885, noted in his first annual report, "In the absence of anything definite as to the employment of the convicts engaged in that way, I will be a little perplexed in finding work for them, which I must do to keep them from idleness. I hope a solution of this vexed matter may soon be satisfactorily reached."

Such a solution was found a few years later in a major reconstruction plan for the penitentiary. For a time the men would be put to work rebuilding and enhancing their prison, work that their predecessors had begun more than fifty years before. These projects included building the Prison of Isolation, where difficult, incorrigible and dangerous inmates could be segregated, later known as the East Cell Block (ECB in prison jargon) and now simply as the Treatment Centre; reconstructing all cell blocks to meet the

standards of the day; and erecting an eighty seven foot tall water tower for the penitentiary, a "sightly structure of partially dressed stone, showing some slight architectural taste" according to Warden Lavell. This tower is now the property of Queen's University, but still to be seen north of the penitentiary, past the Prison for Women, which would also be built with convict labour in the early 1930s. By the beginning of the twentieth century Kingston Penitentiary presented a markedly different appearance than at the time of its opening in 1835. It was bigger. It was stronger. It had been lived in, and died in. It was permanent.

FACTORIES TO REMAKE MEN

In 1920, the Superintendent of Penitentiaries said in his annual report: "Penitentiaries are now fast being regarded as industrics/factories to manufacture government material and to remake men. From depraved, neglected, diseased and crooked materials received, their object is to turn out, as their product, good citizens, reformed and fully qualified to take their places in the world of work."

It was a daunting assignment, and there were many failures. Indeed, there were more failures than successes, for the rate of recidivism remained as high as it had ever been. There are those who believe that once a criminal has progressed far enough in anti-social behaviour to merit a term in federal penitentiary, there is little likelihood of his ever making an honest recovery and returning to normal society. It is certainly possible, but the odds count against it. Well over half the inmates of Kingston Penitentiary throughout the years of its existence, have been repeat offenders. They get out, but they find it difficult to stay out. One of the greatest problems for ex-convicts is to find jobs and a livelihood on the outside, particularly in times of economic hardship.

The factory production line at Kingston Penitentiary in the Twenties was a sign of the times and a reflection of the economic and social organization of the day. The penitentiary factory would use inmate labour to manufacture products for internal government needs. In this way it might avoid the fate of its predecessor, the contract system, which practised open competition with the private sector and floundered because of it. In the first half of the twentieth

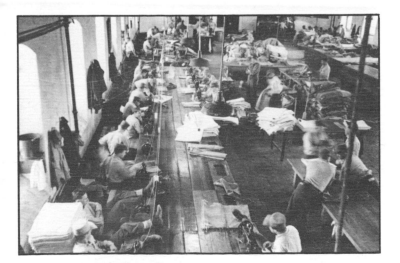

century the factory concept predominated in Kingston Penitentiary.

One of the outstanding and most successful examples of the factory system at Kingston Penitentiary is the mailbag manufacture and repair shop, which opened in the 1870's and has operated continuously ever since. In 1923, revenue in the mailbag department was $27,000. A year later it had leaped to $37,000. In that year, about 100,000 new bags had been manufactured for the Post Office, about the same number of defective bags repaired, and a little custom work done for penitentiary officers, including seven school bags, two horse blankets and five hammocks. Its turnover exceeded the volume in the tailoring and shoemaking shops combined. Mailbags from every corner of the world have made their way to this shop for repair. It has been a constant source of employment, filling a useful role, helping to defray operational costs.

THE WAR YEARS

During the two world wars, the factory system continued. Kingston Penitentiary was an arm of the war effort, since the prison shops manufactured items essential to the operation of the government. Some of the tailoring capacity was turned to making uniforms for soldiers. In general, though, the normal production routine was followed, since it was already geared to government requirements.

The routine of the penitentiary hardly changes to take war into account, even world wars. The population tends to decline briefly as war work opens up and alternative means of channeling aggressive behaviour are given the sanction of military necessity. Kingston Penitentiary had a population of five hundred and eleven

convicts in 1914, more than a quarter of the 2,003 prisoners in Canada's seven penitentiaries (Alberta, opened in 1906 but closed in 1920, and Saskatchewan, opened at Prince Albert in 1911, were a new generation of Kingston Penitentiary descendants, joining the four bastilles built in the 1870s). When the First World War ended in 1918, Kingston Penitentiary's population was down to four hundred and thirteen out of 1,463 federal prisoners across the country, the lowest count in more than a decade. At the height of hostilities in 1944, the count was six hundred and forty five out of the Canadian total of 3,078 federal prisoners, down from eight hundred and fourteen out of 3,552 ten years earlier, at the depths of the Great Depression.

NEW EMPHASIS ON EDUCATION AND TRAINING

In the post-war period of the late 1940s, increasing emphasis was placed on education and training for inmates. There were several reasons. It was a legitimate activity that filled the time of men whose greatest enemy was the tedium of prison life. It could be a substitute for work, of which there was not a great deal after the limited demand of the government for mail boxes, mailbags, shelves and metal desks was filled. And it held the promise of providing a means for inmates to improve their skills and their chances. By 1957, Kingston Penitentiary inmates were involved in over two hundred and fifty educational programs. While the mailbag repair operation continued, virtually every other program reflected the changing times. Academic and vocational training predominated, adding a new dimension to penitentiary work, and the

learning, skills upgrading, secondary education and, through correspondence, university training. Inmates continue to be employed in maintaining the penitentiary and providing for their own daily needs. Many work as cleaners, electricians, plumbers and groundskeepers to help keep the institution humming. Much of the work inside the walls has changed dramatically since 1835. Much remains as it always was, given only the general changes that society and technology have brought to the massive enclosure that rises formidably on the point jutting into the great lake.

insistence on hard physical labour faded to memory.

But an impressive variety of activity has been maintained. The South Block, under an impressive vaulted dome, houses a furniture upholstery shop, vocational barber shop, and an information processing centre where inmates are taught the use of computer terminals and programs, then given the chance to try their newly acquired skills on government data entry and other program applications.

The Kingston Penitentiary school area offers a comprehensive curriculum of remedial basic

A BIRD'S EYE VIEW

In essence, the routine on the inside is ordained by the nature of the institution. It is in a bit of a time warp even as the world changes. Kingston Penitentiary once had Hatter's Bay to its west. In 1976 the bay was renamed Portsmouth Harbour and rebuilt as a world-class marina. It became the site of yachting competition for the Olympic Games, which were held that year in Montréal and Kingston. Inmates with cells on upper tiers can see over the walls. They had a bird's-eye view of one of the world's great sporting events. They had nowhere to go. The Olympics came to them. As was to be expected, however, in an environment where nothing is the same as in the free society outside the limestone walls, the Games were not universally welcomed by Kingston Penitentiary inhabitants. Not every inmate wants an upper tier cell. There are many who do not care to be reminded of what they are missing on the outside. They find it easier to "shake" the time that way.

Attitudes, methods and techniques have changed, as society and its understanding of criminality have evolved, as even the landscape is reshaped with the seasons, with the years, with the uses of new generations. But the goals of staff at Kingston Penitentiary have remained remarkably consistent. They want to keep secure the inmates entrusted to them by the justice system and to give each one as much assistance as the system allows, and the offender will accept, to work his way back to a free society.

CHAPTER VI

KINGSTON PENITENTIARY
AND
THE COMMUNITY

KINGSTON PENITENTIARY AND THE COMMUNITY

Everywhere in Canada there are people who think of Kingston as penitentiary city. The penitentiary is imbedded in the culture, the commerce and the consciousness of the community. From the very earliest days, when it was taking shape as one of Canada's largest public buildings, Kingston Penitentiary has been hard to ignore.

PORTSMOUTH HAD THE EDGE

It has been a constant and considerable factor in local employment and investment. There was hardly any settled population at Portsmouth, where few homes were standing before the penitentiary was contemplated. The penitentiary immediately became a source of employment and the village grew, first as a dormitory for construction workers, later filling with residences for the permanent staff within the walls. The population and the village grew with Kingston Penitentiary. Officially called the Provincial Penitentiary at its beginning, it was known locally as Portsmouth Penitentiary and is still called that sometimes, even though it was rechristened Kingston Penitentiary at Confederation in 1867.

A local directory for 1857 shows twenty nine householders in Portsmouth Village employed at the penitentiary, including the chaplain and the messenger. There was a total staff of sixty three at the time, and a convict population of over seven hundred.

Portsmouth had an edge on penitentiary jobs because, for more than a century, one of the conditions of employment at Kingston Penitentiary was that officers must live within sound of the penitentiary bell. The bell was rung twice daily, at the start and the close of the day, after the inmate count was in and correct, as a signal that staff could leave and to give assurance to the community that "all is well" within the walls. For the villagers the afternoon bell meant that the convicts were secure within their cells for the night. The practice of ringing the bell at the day's opening and closing continues to the present. Its purpose now is more symbolic, since staff may live many miles beyond hearing range. (Another

bell, or gong, also reverberated inside the walls, as described in Chapter VIII.)

BEAUP'S TAVERN

The name Beaupré has been associated with the Portsmouth area for many generations. A family member was on the original town council. The Portsmouth Tavern, originally Beaupré's Tavern, opened in 1860 on the west shore of Hatter's Bay, a good snowball throw from Tower Three in the centre of Kingston Penitentiary's west wall. It is still regarded as the local by many off-shift penitentiary officers. Even though its name has changed, often it is referred to as Beaup's. Oldtimers remember its back room, reserved for guards, policemen and bus drivers, who for many years were forbidden to appear in any drinking establishment while in uniform. There are few annual reports of Kingston Penitentiary with lists of staff in the past century and a half that do not contain the name of at least one member of the Beaupré family.

"VISITORS BREED DISCONTENT"

Kingston Penitentiary has always been a great attraction for visitors to the city. Today most tourists only see the prison fortress from King Street, which runs along the penitentiary's front wall from Tower One at the northeast corner, past the North Gate, and on beyond Tower Two at the northwest corner. But until well into the twentieth century visitors could tour the penitentiary by paying a fee at the front gate.

This arrangement was a constant source of annoyance to Warden and staff, and to the inmates who had to suffer the ignominy of being exhibited in a human zoo as well as their already considerable punishment.

In his annual report for 1902, Warden J. Platt expressed the following concerns regarding visitors:

"The Admission of visitors to the Penitentiary is, under existing regulations, the cause of much trouble and annoyance to the Warden, and some dissatisfaction among the inmates. There is an ever-increasing army of tourists, excursionists and general sightseers who throng our cities during the summer months . . .Ninety-nine hundredths of those who apply for admission, and nine-tenths of those who are admitted, have no interest in the institution and are drawn thither either by a morbid curiosity or an unexplainable desire to gaze upon the unfortunate confined within its walls. I consider it monstrous cruelty to place convicts upon exhibition before men, women, boys and girls, and I do not blame them for resenting it. Thus, the admission of visitors interferes with discipline, no matter how circumspectly visitors may conduct themselves. Besides, it must not be forgotten that many convicts have mothers and wives and sisters and children at home, and that painful thoughts and emotions and yearning for home and freedom are often aroused by sight of those who, in size, age, appearance or carriage, resemble their own loved ones. Thus, the admission of visitors breeds discontent . . . The Prison is, or should be, a place of industry. It is not a zoo, nor a menagerie, nor a free show of any kind. In this institution, we are as busy as the inmates of any factory or industrial establishment,

Portsmouth Penitentiary, Kingston, Ontario, Canada.-25A

The Penitentiary, Kingston, Ontario, Canada. -32

Provincial Penitentiary, Kingston, Ont.

and we cannot afford to keep two or three officers at the gate ready to conduct visitors."

The practice of permitting tourists to wander throughout the prison has ceased, but the institution continues to be one of Kingston's major tourist attractions. One indication of the public's interest in Kingston Penitentiary is the number of postcard messages it inspires. "Wish you were here" is a sentiment written by thousands of people on cards depicting the historic penitentiary, and these continue to be best sellers.

MEDIA CRITICISM

Kingston is home not only to the first federal penitentiary in Canada, but also to Canada's oldest continuously-published daily newspaper. The Kingston Whig Standard, formerly the Daily British Whig, has always taken a great interest in Kingston Penitentiary and continues to devote much space to events taking place in and around it. It is hardly surprising that an institution which has housed Canada's most notorious criminals for a hundred and fifty years, at taxpayer's expense, attracts active interest from press and public. The media in general have never been reticent about commenting on conditions and events in the penitentiary, not always supported by knowledge of the facts.

Criticism by the press went with the job, but sometimes it rankled particularly hard and penitentiary authorities would retaliate with whatever weapons they had at their disposal. The Inspectors of Penitentiaries, Douglas Stewart and W.S. Hughes, spoke up this way in 1913, writing: "During the past year the Penitentiaries have been subjected to more than their usual quota of criticism. It is needless to state that fair constructive criticism is welcomed as helpful and receives careful consideration by those engaged in the task of administering penal institutions. There is a class of criticism, however, which is merely the parrot-like reiteration of mis-statements of officials who have violated their oath of office, or the equally unreliable vapourings of ex-convicts who seek notoriety. Such criticism is unfair and injurious. There is no closed season to protect officials from such attacks. They can do so only in their annual reports."

THE PENITENTIARY NEIGHBOURHOOD

Prospective residents often ask about the effect that a penitentiary has on real estate values. Kingston Penitentiary's imposing presence does not seem to have collided with some of the more prestigious housing in the city of Kingston. Kingston Penitentiary is massive. It may be possible, however, for a non-resident to drive by and mistake it for another public warehouse. It does not scare the Queen's University students who jog by it every day, nor the younger children who pass it on the way to school. Most of the residences to the north and east of the penitentiary were planned and built after Kingston Penitentiary was already there. Alwington Place, for example, which is just east of the penitentiary, is today generally considered to be one of the more desirable of the city's residential areas. Close neighbours have included three Governors-General and at least one Mayor in addition to many prominent community leaders. When just a Kingston lawyer, John A. Macdonald lived nearby at Bellevue House, which is now a national historic site.

GOODS AND SERVICES FOR THE PENITENTIARY

In addition to many jobs created inside the walls, the penitentiary has been a major customer for local merchants and tradesmen. The earliest general accounts show disbursements to dozens of Kingston suppliers for quantities of indian meal, charcoal, bread and flour, lumber, cordwood, oak scantling, hardwares, cottons, leather, beef, tin ware, potatoes, stationery and printing, straw, salt, bibles, medicines, molasses,

meal and peas, socks, soap and candles, flannel, sand, old copper, yeast, firewood, drawing paper, bricks, milk, deer skins, oil, haygrass, tallow, beeswax, lead pencils, glass, gunpowder and advertising. The annual report for 1852 includes a bewildering variety of goods and services purchased in the community, everything from five shillings for "digging a grave" to $807.92 to E. Chanteloup for "repairing kettles". Details of spending ran to a dozen columns of fine type in the 1916 annual report, for more than seven hundred kinds of items. By the mid-Twenties, Kingston Penitentiary was spending more than $400,000 a year, half for salaries and employee benefits and the rest for supplies. Ten years later the figure was just over $500,000. By the mid-Fifties it had reached $1.5 million. At the centennial of Confederation in 1967, the penitentiary payroll and purchases amounted to just over $3 million a year.

INMATES AS NEIGHBOURS

In earlier days, inmates of Kingston Penitentiary were much more visible in the community than they are today. Until well into the twentieth century the penitentiary lands covered several hundred acres which extended northward as far as Princess Street (Highway #2), encompassing a large farm as well as a quarry operation. For many years inmates would parade through Portsmouth Village in their unmistakable striped uniforms. They were always escorted by armed officers on horseback, on their way to a day of work in the prison quarries or on the farm. This was a routine sight for residents of the area, who often came to know some of their neighbours from the big house on King Street.

Bill Westlake, former Senior Deputy Commissioner of the Correctional Service, was born in Portsmouth. His father worked at the penitentiary for over thirty years. Mr. Westlake has many memories of his childhood in the village, including this one:

"Inmates of Kingston Penitentiary were neighbours, sometimes our friends, but always part of the community. We saw them working the fields, in and around the grounds of the institution and through the quarry located in the village. I remember quite clearly a number of the inmates who we saw on a regular basis. There was an old recidivist named Slim Summerville who was known to all the kids in the village. As the quarry gang marched back and forth each day Slim could be found bringing up the tail end. The village kids often ran along the road carrying on a conversation with the inmates. Old Slim was a particular favourite and he, in turn, seemed to appreciate and show affection to those of us who ran along beside the gang.

"I also have very vivid recollections of Canada's Public Enemy No. 1 in the 1920s, Red Ryan (whose tale had many facets, another of which is examined in Chapter IX). On the occasion of his discharge from Kingston, my father was the acting messenger, and I accompanied him as he transported Red to the train station on the date of his release. I remember very clearly Mr. Ryan handing me a dime to buy a candy bar or an ice cream cone. Shortly after, Red Ryan was shot and killed while attempting to rob a bank.

"Amazingly, those of us who lived in the village did not perceive these inmates as hardened criminals, but rather just another branch of the community in which we resided. I grew up in an atmosphere and environment where penitentiary inmates were an accepted part of our daily life pattern."

CHANGES INSIDE THE WALLS

But agriculture and limestone production gradually gave way to the encroachment of the city. Housing developments covered the fields and the quarries. Kingston Penitentiary inmates no longer had reason to walk outside the walls.

Today they are cut off from the outside world from the moment they walk through the forbidding North Gate. Taken on arrival to the old Northwest Cell Block, once the quarters for

women prisoners inside the penitentiary, they are searched, showered, disinfected, interviewed, photographed, clothed. They hand over the personal effects they have with them. A form is filled out, which the inmate must sign below the line that reads, "The above is a correct list of all the articles received with the body of inmate X."

One column on the form is for "articles condemned or burnt with inmates consent or by order." Some things may be bagged and stored for their release. But it is preferable to send valuables on to a mother or wife, because there is some pilferage in penitentiary, where there are many thieves. Then the new arrival will be locked inside for a long time. Inmates are not sent to Kingston Penitentiary, or any other federal penitentiary, unless they have been sentenced to at least two years. Anything less would be served in a provincial prison.

As occasions for outside work dwindled, diverse activities to fill time were slowly being introduced inside the walls. Silent films produced by government agencies were shown starting in 1923, but these soon ended when talking pictures came along and the government balked at the high cost of new projection equipment. Until 1933 radios were not permitted, and even when they were, music and censored programs broadcast by CBC were allowed, but only for one hour on Sunday afternoons. This policy has since been much

relaxed. Today inmates run their own internal station inside the penitentiary, wired into the cell blocks. Many inmates are able to watch programs on television sets in their own cells, a privilege they can earn by work and attitude. A TV set in every cell might seem like prison pampering on the outside, but veteran officers say it is the greatest aid to

inmate control since tear gas. TV gives inmates a way other than mind games and mayhem to occupy their time.

ENTERTAINMENT AND SPORTING EVENTS

The community has always been ready to bring entertainment and self-improvement sessions in from the outside. As late as 1927 permission was refused to bring educational lecturers in, but this attitude was soon to be relaxed. In 1933 a concert a month was permitted in winter, with male performers only. Probably the first entertainers were choral groups and bands, often from the Salvation Army, who performed at Christmas and Easter.

In 1945, Joe Woodhouse, a local businessman and piano player, began rounding up groups of entertainers for Sunday variety shows at Kingston Penitentiary. The performers included a young impressionist from Ottawa, Rich Little, Billy O'Connor, and a perennial favorite, Katie Murtaugh, who was known as Canada's Sophie Tucker, in addition to many local musicians, singers and comedians. It was all a volunteer effort by the entertainers, to bring some cheer and hope to the men inside. Private individuals and voluntary organizations have made great contributions to penitentiary life over the time that society has used incarceration to punish criminals. Kingston Penitentiary has seen many of them.

Penitentiary inmates have put together some excellent sporting events over the years, including boxing exhibitions, track and field days, soccer tournaments. Baseball teams have played in the Kingston area league. This was somewhat unfair to opposing teams, of course, since all of the Kingston Penitentiary games had to be played at home. Invited spectators remember games at the penitentiary diamond in the 1950s. It was a little intimidating to be confronted with as many as a thousand inmate fans, all cheering wildly for their home team.

"MAKING GOOD" WITH A LITTLE HELP

Not all of the community visitors to Kingston Penitentiary have been tourists, tap dancers or shortstops. Inmates and prison officers alike are in the debt of the many individuals and agencies who have devoted themselves to assisting prisoners. One of the earliest John Howard

Society members to visit on a regular basis was the late J. Alex Edmison, former president of the Canadian Penal Association and assistant to the principal of Queen's University. Edmison was vitally interested in all matters related to the criminal justice system and wrote many papers and articles on the topic of penal reform.

In 1954, Alex Edmison wrote in the magazine, **Historic Kingston:**

"Today, in Kingston Penitentiary, prisoners are people. The results of this new approach are already apparent. I count among my friends many discharges who are "making good" and are a credit to their country. There is always tragedy present when the shackled individuals are ushered off the train at Kingston station en route to the Penitentiary. That so many of them can afterwards emerge therefrom with hope for the future is perhaps the most important thing one can now say in dealing with the History of Kingston Penitentiary."

The Salvation Army has always been eager to offer help and advice to inmates and their families. To this day, Sally Ann officers in their familiar uniforms can be seen regularly in the

heart of the penitentiary, distributing copies of **The War Cry** and helping in the many ways which have gained them such respect around the world. In 1897, Warden Metcalfe gave permission to the Salvation Army to conduct four meetings annually at the penitentiary. During the same year, Major Mrs. Blanche Read was among the first women to preach to inmates inside the penitentiary. In her book, **The Lady With the Other Lamp**, she writes of this visit:

"What a sight met our eyes as we stepped to the reading desk. To the right was the great organ - skillfully played through the service by the splendid organist - and about thirty men who formed the choir seated on slightly elevated seats. To the left, in a little closet-like room the few women prisoners sat. Before us, a sea of faces - men old and furrowed, middle-aged men whose wives and children were deprived of a husband and father's love and protection.

"Young men were amongst the number, with bright intelligent, alert faces and faces of a duller cast. Eighty men serving life sentences!

"Boys too - quite a crowd of boys - youths who through strong drink, or under the stress of sore temptation, had fallen in the fowler's snare."

In 1985, volunteers walk through the North Gate every evening to help in group sessions, including Alcoholics Anonymous, John Howard Society, Native Brotherhood, Dale Carnegie training, religious organizations, French cultural groups and many more. One of the more recent examples of community interaction with the penitentiary is the Citizen's Advisory Committee, a group of volunteer appointees who advise the Warden on the general management of the

prison. This dedicated group meets as well with inmates and staff. Members tour the penitentiary and sometimes are asked to provide assistance during emergency situations.

When the penitentiary was being built in 1834, on the east shore of Hatter's Bay, it appeared on Kingston city maps only as an arrow pointing west off the chart, marked "to the Penitentiary". Since then the city has grown around it and it has become part of Kingston. King Street, once a dirt road leading to the penitentiary and Portsmouth, has seen horsedrawn carriages and streetcars, the electric railway and automobiles, all passing in front of the silent, stately, limestone structure which has blended into the shoreline as though it were just another fine example of the city's old stonework.

CHAPTER VII

WOMEN IN THE PENITENTIARY

WOMEN IN THE PENITENTIARY

Women were imprisoned at Kingston Penitentiary for the first hundred years.

Three female prisoners arrived in September 1835, much to the surprise of Warden Smith, who was aware that females would eventually be housed at Kingston Penitentiary but did not expect they would arrive so soon. Susan Turner, Hannah Downes and Hannah Baglen, all serving one to two years for larceny, were housed temporarily in the hospital until a separate facility could be found. This accommodation was to last until 1839, when part of the North Wing was designated as the first prison for women.

During his visit to Kingston Penitentiary in 1842, Charles Dickens was particularly struck by the female convicts. "Among them was a beautiful girl of twenty, who had been there nearly three years. She acted as bearer of secret dispatches for the self-styled patriots of Navy Island, during the Canadian Insurrection sometimes dressing as a girl, and carrying them in her stays; sometimes attiring herself as a boy, and secreting them in the lining of her hat. In the latter character she always rode as a boy would, which was nothing for her, for she could govern any horse that any man could ride, and could drive a four-in-hand with the best whip in those parts. Setting forth on one of her patriotic missions, she appropriated to herself the first horse she could get her hands on; and this offence brought her where I saw her. She had quite a lovely face, though, as the reader may suppose from this sketch of her history, there was a lurking devil in her bright eye, which looked pretty sharply from between her prison bars." (This young woman was probably Eunice Whiting who was serving three years for horse stealing.)

"A WRETCHED MAKESHIFT"

By 1858 the female inmates had moved several times, always outgrowing their space. The Warden reports that year that eight women prisoners were forced to sleep in the corridor. There were not enough cells to go around. At the same time, the Inspectors were saying in their report that "Female prisons should never be within the boundary walls of other prisons." It would be more than seventy years before that recommendation was realized.

At the time of Confederation, the female convict population had grown to sixty and the Inspector's report in 1867 strongly advocated the building of a proper female prison outside the walls of Kingston Penitentiary, either on land to be purchased to the east, or on prison land to the north. The only decision made at the time was to ignore the recommendation about buying more land. It was not bought, and the proposed site eventually developed into a prestigeous residential community.

More than twenty years later, in 1889, Inspector James G. Moylan said of the accommodation for women: "I have always considered this portion of the penitentiary unfit for the use that is made of it. Apart from its objectionable proximity to the male prison, the cells being underground in a gloomy and dismal compartment is sufficient cause for recommending a change." Four years later he spoke of the facilities as being "a wretched makeshift" so far as the cells and laundry were concerned.

ALTERNATIVES FOR HOUSING WOMEN PRISONERS

In 1909 it was decided to construct a separate prison for women, but still it was to be located within the walls of Kingston Penitentiary. Male convicts were set to work to construct the building. In February 1913, the females moved into their new quarters, the Northwest Cell Block, just to the right of the North Gate and still in use at Kingston Penitentiary as the reception and processing centre for arriving inmates.

The following year, the Royal Commission on Penitentiaries commented favorably on the new building. "Yet," the commissioners said, "it should be stated that the interests of all concerned would be best served if those few inmates were transferred to an institution for women. It may be possible that, as has been suggested elsewhere in this report, in connection with certain other classes, arrangements might be made with the Provincial authorities for the custody of all female offenders."

The recommendation that the provinces handle female offenders, thus allowing them to serve time closer to home, was to be repeated many times in the ensuing years. There are provincial facilities in all parts of Canada for women inmates, to house those who are sentenced by the courts to less than two years. There are many more women incarcerated by the provinces than federally. But in 1985 most anglophone female inmates are still housed at the Prison for Women in Kingston. The majority of francophone women, however, are held in Maison Tanguay, a provincial institution in Québec, under a contractual agreement between that province and the federal government. While agreements with some provinces are now in effect, no satisfactory arrangement has been made to date with all of them which would allow the only federal institution for women to close its doors.

The Northwest Cell Block contained thirty two regular cells and two double sick-bay cells. Within a few years it was overcrowded, with a population of forty inmates. In 1920, a report to the Minister of Justice reiterated that, "Women convicts should be confined in a completely separate institution out of view of the male penitentiary." A subsequent report to the Minister recommended that a new prison be built "outside and away a bit from the male prison."

A NEW PRISON FOR WOMEN

When construction began on the present Prison for Women (known as P4W) in May 1925, using convict labour, ground was broken north of Kingston Penitentiary, behind the Warden's residence. For a number of years, the Kingston Penitentiary Warden was also responsible for P4W, which was first occupied by female inmates on January 24, 1934. It had already been in use for about a year to house an overflow of male inmates from Kingston Penitentiary.

After ninety nine years, women were finally moved beyond the confines of the male institution. They had been housed in a temporary

hospital, a "wretched makeshift", and an overcrowded building. Now they had their own prison, just a short distance from where the first three arrived and were promptly put in the custody of Kingston Penitentiary's original Matron, Mrs. Elmherst.

Matron has always been an important figure at the penitentiary. In his 1845 annual report, the chaplain at Kingston Penitentiary suggested that she "should bear a relative position to the Warden himself, since much must necessarily depend on

her, in which, even that superior Officer cannot, with propriety, be consulted." Chaplain R.J. Rogers also felt that she should, by her character, deportment and education, "be raised to such an eminence, as that the unhappy convict may look up to her as an example; and command obedience by moral influence, rather than physical force."

The conviction that women are the best guardians of other women remains part of the penitentiary system today. There are no male guards on female ranges at P4W. At the all-male Kingston Penitentiary, on the other hand, there

are female officers in evidence everywhere. Mary Dawson was appointed Warden in September, 1984. This is very new in what had been an impenetrable male bastion, and a big step forward from the days of Matron. There were many fine Matrons at Kingston Penitentiary in the old days. Despite the chaplain's good offices, they were never in the running to become Warden.

THE PENAL PRESS

The mid-twentieth century was the heyday of the inmate publication **Telescope.** Females figured prominently in putting the magazine together. It was a creative era at Kingston Penitentiary, demonstrated by the remarkable variety of crafts and arts produced by inmates.

Telescope was one of America's best written and illustrated examples of the "penal press" of the day. It tried to publish twelve issues a year, although the schedule was subject to disruption by any disturbances inside, ranging from escape rumours to the full scale riot of 1954 (described in Chapter X). Subscribers all across Canada and the United States paid a dollar a year to receive it. Coca Cola advertised on the back cover. The magazine's inmate editors put together a brief for the Canadian Bar Association in 1955. Of the ten inmates on the editorial staff in 1961, five were women. At the time there were just under a thousand male inmates at Kingston Penitentiary and just over a hundred females at P4W.

The evidence indicates that, to a limited extent, women and men inmates have always been able to communicate with each other at Kingston Penitentiary. One of the first discoveries noted by Warden Michael Lavell in his journal, in February 1886, was that letters were passing between male and female convicts. In the 1960s,

staff discovered bound and waterproofed cigarette packs stuffed with messages and flushed in sewage from P4W down to an outlet catchment under Kingston Penitentiary at the lake, where they could be retrieved by male inmates on the plumbing crews. But there is no evidence that inmates of opposite sexes have ever had physical contact. Several babies have been born to female inmates at Kingston Penitentiary in its long history, but the pregnancies had begun before admittance. In some cases, infants were allowed to stay with mothers in their cells. But only up to a certain age. If the mother's sentence was too long, and a pardon or parole denied, the child would be sent to an orphanage or, if lucky, to a relative or foster home. Almost anything was considered preferable to growing up in a prison environment. The child deserved a better chance than that.

GOOD ORDER AND INDUSTRY

During their century within Kingston Penitentiary walls, strictly separated from the men but occasionally in glimpsing distance, female prisoners were engaged in the manufacture of inmate clothing and other needlework activities. The report of Matron Mary Leahy of 1872 records that, "The earnings of the female convicts as shown in the labour returns, amount to $1,560.20, the cash receipts to $684.40, being $244.39 in excess of last year." Among the items manufactured were two hundred and one aprons, thirty four sun bonnets, four hundred and six pillowcases and 1,480 pair of socks.

By the following year, the female population had fallen to only fifteen. Mrs. Leahy was happy to report that her charges had spent only fourteen days in solitary confinement on a diet of bread and water during the entire year. In 1881, the women were manufacturing grey flannel shirts for the Indian Department and the North West Mounted Police. Mrs. Leahy expressed her delight with the good order and industry of the "comparatively few" women in the prison.

The number of female convicts stayed very low for a number of years. At the turn of the century there were some facilities for women prisoners at Edmonton and Dorchester institutions, but these were phased out during the First World War. In 1915 Mary Leahy's successor, Matron Rose Fahey, who first took charge of females at Kingston Penitentiary in 1886, reported that she had twenty five convicts in her custody, "nine received from Edmonton." The year before, there had been only ten women at the penitentiary, which was the more usual size of population. Matron Fahey never had as many as forty staying with her at once. In fact they did stay together. The Matron had living quarters on the upper floor of the Northwest Cell Block.

The problem of finding enough work for women was just as persistent as it was for men. In 1918 it was eased somewhat when the Red Cross provided materials that the convicts processed into bandages and other articles needed in the war effort. It was the start of a relationship that would continue at Kingston Penitentiary in various ways. In the mid-Sixties, for instance, Red Cross blood donor clinics were set up inside the walls twice a year. In 1966, though the total prison population never exceeded eight hundred and seventy five, the clinics collected nine hundred and ninety pints of blood from inmates at Kingston Penitentiary, eleven percent of the Red Cross quota for all of Kingston.

THE MATRONS

The Matrons' fortunes had their ups and downs. They were paid less than the male officers. In 1914, when the Warden was getting $2,800 a year and the lowest-paid guard was earning $800, Matron Fahey's salary after nearly thirty years of service was $700. Ten years later her successor's salary had been raised to $1,140. This was below the top of the salary scale for guards, but at least it was slightly above the bottom of the scale.

Just as it did for male officers, a change of Warden sometimes meant a sharp re-assessment of a Matron's competence and contribution, no matter how long and faithful her service. Matron Fahey held her appointment through the tenures of five Wardens. She had arrived just after the death of John Creighton, and received commendations from all of his successors up to and including Warden Robert Creighton, his son, who wrote in 1918 that the female ward at Kingston Penitentiary was "admirably managed by intelligent and faithful Matrons." The next year Creighton was transferred to headquarters in Ottawa. Warden J.C. Ponsford, who had previously run the federal penitentiaries in

Manitoba and Alberta, took a different view. He forced the resignations of Rose Fahey and her deputy, alleging that affairs in the women's prison "had not been at all satisfactorily managed."

BLISTERS, CUTS AND BROKEN NAILS

At the new P4W the work shortage problem was attacked by putting a poultry house in the enclosure, by encouraging hobbycraft and, in the summer, small kitchen gardens. In her column in **Telescope** for July 1955, inmate Della Burns catches some of the flavour of the activity: "The garden-minded gals are combining business with pleasure these days, enjoying old Sol while digging and planting. Irene and Maria spend all their spare time in their plots and have already transplanted several plants. Overheard Nonie comment that she could honestly write home about working on the rock pile! A gem of truth! Blisters, cuts and broken nails are all part of the spoils — the better part is eagerly awaited! Many thanks to Miss Patterson for bringing us seeds and to Mrs. Greer for her tomato plants; they are much appreciated by all the farmerettes."

Life was not all roses, by any means. Women did hard time too. The Brown Commission reported in 1849 that girls as young as twelve were lashed repeatedly for the same trifling offences as boys. Corporal punishment continued for females as long as it did for males. Strapping was finally abolished only in 1972, though it had been abandoned in practice five years earlier.

One thing the farmerettes did not appreciate was any damage to their clothing. Female inmates in 1985 may wear their own clothing. But this is a recent privilege. For most of their time at Kingston Penitentiary and P4W women have had to get along with prison garb. Naomi Green, who took over as women's columnist for **Telescope** when Del Burns was released, wrote in the September 1959 issue: "On admission each girl is issued two dresses — that's what they call them, anyway. The girls who work in the kitchen or hospital are issued white dresses. The rest of us get the blue and white jobs with the vertical stripes. If necessary, one dress a year is issued to replace a discard. But to obtain a new garment one has really to have an attorney to represent her."

In 1983 some women were returned to Kingston Penitentiary to a separate wing of the Treatment Centre. A new program to improve psychological treatment for inmates from P4W was begun at that time in what was seen as a major step to give women in prison access to therapy and rehabilitation counselling that they had lacked over the years.

CHAPTER VIII

DOING TIME

DOING TIME

Kingston Penitentiary became Canada's big house in the public mind during the mid-twentieth century. It was an image fostered by the spate of Hollywood gangster movies of the day featuring stars such as Cagney, Robinson and Bogart.

The penitentiary presented a formidable façade to the public. Regular tours had long since been abandoned. There was little way of knowing what went on within those walls. A strict military discipline prevailed. However, as the century progressed, changed in public attitudes towards authority and personal self-expression brought profound changes in the prison.

WORK AND RIGOROUS ROUTINE

We have a detailed look at life in Kingston Penitentiary in the early 1920s. A reporter from the Toronto Star Weekly was permitted to tour the facility and spend some time there. His article provides a snapshot of the daily routine.

We see a prison firmly committed to reformation through discipline. The main instrument of that discipline was work and a rigorous routine.

Cleanliness was sacred. All inmates worked under instructor guards who provided both training and supervision of the labour. Warden J.D. Ponsford was the epitome of the all-powerful, distant, yet compassionate custodian. As the article says, "To the Warden is due the present morale of the Prison and the strict discipline, the penal realities, the humane reformative opportunity to work and the chance to study, blended in such proportions as to make the inmate appreciate if he is capable, that, although a prisoner expiating a crime against society, he is still a man."

In the Warden's view, "Indolence puts ninety percent of the men in the Penitentiary. Indolence pure and simple. Not drink or drugs. A man would not be looking for drink or dope or any of the forty other things blamed for crime if it were not for indolence . . . To every newcomer who stands before me I preach the doctrine of work, work and more work. Then he is asked, 'What trade would you like to learn?' "

Guided by this very clear view of his job, Warden Ponsford was instrumental in industrializing the penitentiary.

BELLS, BELLS AND MORE BELLS

To ensure the productivity of his shops and control of the prison, Warden Ponsford enforced a strict régime. Symbolic of the rules and the precise scheduling of the day's events was the bell in the Main Dome, which signalled the beginning and end of all activities. This gong became a symbol of oppression and regimentation to the inmates.

Even then, guards and keepers were commonly called "screws" by the inmates. The Deputy Warden in charge of operations and security, who in that day was R.R. Tucker, was known as the "screwdriver". It was upon his command that the gong was rung and the movement of inmates begun. From the reporter's account: "Then the prison came to life. The Deputy Warden pulls the gong again. Keys rattle. Guards move swiftly. Range barriers swing open. The windlasses on each line of cells throw every bolt into gear. The gong again. The first cell of each line opens. The inmate, the *tapper* as he is called, runs to the far end of his line of cells. The gong again.

"From away up on the top line of Range A comes the sound of a man running and a quick tap-tap-tap as he speeds along. As he runs, he strikes each protruding bolt a blow with his open hand as he passes. In seconds, he unlocks the line of cells. The inmates are all standing at their cell barriers at this point and when the sound of the tapping stops, they all open their doors, form a line and proceed to their place of work. They do this silently. No staff speak either. Except for the gong, there is no sound but the shuffling of feet."

Over the years, the penetrating reverberation of the gong came to symbolize the rigid discipline of penitentiary life. There was growing dissatisfaction with this approach to penal servitude, both within the walls and outside. Roger Caron, who served many years in Kingston Penitentiary and won the Governor General's award for literature with **Go Boy**, an account of his experiences in prison, tells of inmate reaction to the sound of the gong in later years:

"To think of Kingston Penitentiary you have to think of the infamous bell. It was right in the center of the circular dome. The dome is like the hub of the wheel. The bell was actually the golden cow for the prison staff. They all gathered around it. It had a platform made of wood, all polished. It was two brass bells one bigger than the other, sitting on each other with a chain dangling from it. You lived and breathed by the bell. When you woke up in the morning the bell rang once and then the lights came on. You had half an hour to get ready for breakfast, get your bunk up against the wall, get your table up against the wall and stand at your door and wait for the tapper to come running down the tier to tap you out. It told you when to eat, when to sleep, when to think: it was just incredible. It drove some people literally crazy. In June 1959, the bell rang in the dome. This guy came charging completely across from A block like a mad enraged bull and butted the bell with his head. I don't know what happened to him but they took him away in a stretcher."

TAKING THE COUNT

In the early 1920s the count of the penitentiary was approximately seven hundred. It continued to grow after that. This could be considered a factor in the troubles that plagued the prison in later years. However, regardless of how many inmates there were, it was necessary to count them several times a day to make sure they were all in their place. From the Keeper's Hall adjacent to the Main Dome area, a complex and intricate count board was maintained. From its inception in the early 1920s to its removal in the 1980s, it remained a source of befuddlement and mystery to those who had not been initiated to its uses.

Its invention is attributed to Deputy Warden Tucker. In action and with practice it was a useful instrument. "On the wall is the check board," reads the description in the Toronto Star. "On this board is a hole corresponding to every cell in the place arranged according to location in tiers and ranges. An empty hole means, at a glance, an occupied cell. A red plug means a man in hospital. A blue plug means a man undergoing punishment. And so on. Every cell in the penitentiary must be checked by the guards on this board and totals made to tally before the all-clear signal rings at night and the prison is sealed tight as the tomb of Tutankhamen."

During this era, prison routine changed little. It was a serviceable system that was geared in discipline and detail to deal with inmates en masse rather than as individuals.

Dress remained essentially the same. Inmates continued to wear a number. Their routine was set forth in the rules and very little disturbed it.

From generation to generation it scarcely deviated. More than thirty years later, in 1960, the Star Weekly sent another reporter to Kingston Penitentiary. He described a typical morning:

"At 6:45 sharp an officer steps to the centre of the concourse to tug a bell once, twice, three times. The sound jolts into every block, range and cell, to be followed by a mass waking up. Coughs, yawns, rustles, sighs — the acoustics are astounding."

A MONOTONOUS ROUTINE

Harvey Blackstock, who was in and out of prisons from coast to coast for a quarter century, wrote in his book **Bitter Humour** that Kingston Penitentiary had a reputation among inmates as the noisiest joint in Canada. He was given a job in the kitchen, a plum assignment, but asked to get out of it because "my nerves just couldn't stand the noise of banging metal trays, shouting, steam hissing, and all the rest of it."

As the typical day begins, each man has a rigid schedule to keep — places to be at certain times, when to eat, sleep, work, relax. The routine is almost as fixed for officers as for inmates. It is numbingly monotonous.

Fifteen minutes after wake-up, the Star report continues,

"the men are presumed to have shaved, washed and dressed. They have toilets and wash basins in their cells. Some don't shave — it isn't compulsory. Some don't dress — they slept in their clothes. Many don't wash.

"They look alike because they dress alike. They wear dark brown jackets with numbers stitched on the backs, heavy boots, thinly striped shirts, light coloured pants. Even now some wear duck bill hats. They are all serving sentences of two years or more, and there the parallel ends. Oldtimers and first offenders, the vicious and the harmless, the illiterate and the genius, the notorious and the unknown, all are thrown together to make up this strange community inside the walls.

"Now the breakfast march begins. The men move slowly, one range following another, to insure a steady flow to the kitchen. They arrive at the kitchen hungry, having last eaten at 4:15 the day before. They

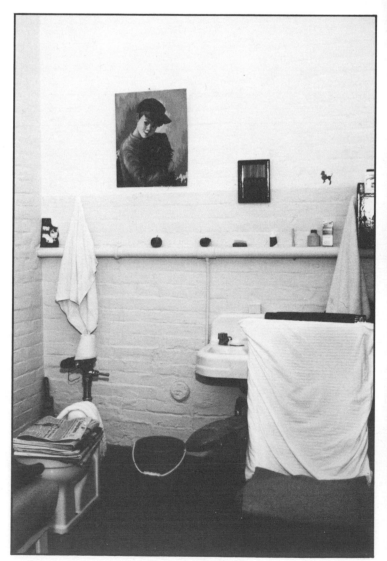

pass along a line to receive oatmeal, milk and sugar, pancakes and syrup, bread, butter, coffee. The menu changes every day and there is no limit to the supply of bread. Most heap their plates with five or six slices. What they don't eat goes to innumerable tame sparrows outside their cells.

"Again columns of men shuffle up the stairs and along the balconies; again guards move about watchfully. Then, another period of silence as the men eat with spoons in their alcoves. The average cell measures ten feet by six. Some contain bare essentials — a cot that folds back, a desk and a chair. Most are more personal, almost like little homes. They have shelves crammed with books, valentines, pictures, Christmas cards, stacks of plywood, tropical fish, leather, embroidery. One cell is called the 'sin bin'. The walls are plastered with pin ups."

THE PRISONER'S PANACEA

What did a man confined to his cell for sixteen hours a day think about? Freedom? Sex? Revenge? The big heist? All of these, perhaps, but

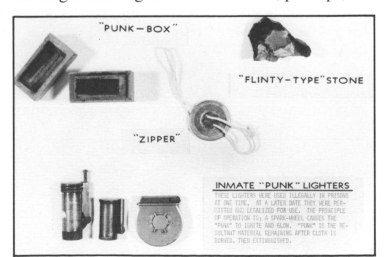

almost certainly he wondered where his next smoke was coming from.

Tobacco was one of the few comforts of prison life. To paraphrase Charles Kingsley, it was the lone man's companion, the bachelor's friend, the hungry man's food, the sad man's cordial, the wakeful man's sleep and the chilly man's fire. In the cashless underground economy of the prison, it was also the universal currency and the most common form of contraband.

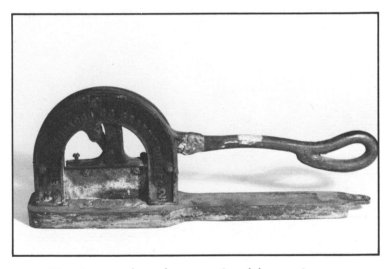

To the penitentiary authorities, tobacco was always a headache. Sometimes they tried to ban it outright, on the grounds that it was immoral, or unsafe, or an unwarranted luxury. Total prohibition, however, was unenforceable.

Most of the time the authorities simply tried to control tobacco use by severely limiting the number of prisoners who could have it, the quantity they could have and the times and places they could indulge in it.

In 1898, for example, Inspector of Penitentiaries Douglas Stewart ordered that "no tobacco is to be given to any convict except on written permission of the surgeon." The only convicts entitled to such a prescription were inmates of the insane ward and prisoners employed on the bucket ground (the sewage disposal area).

But this was an extreme position, even for the time. Wardens considered tobacco an effective tool of discipline. They supplied it as a reward and withdrew it as a punishment.

The ends of discipline were frustrated when inmates could get tobacco from other sources. Tobacco was smuggled into the prison by visitors, and used as an incentive payment by private contractors using prison labour. Guards were so low-paid that they sometimes risked dismissal by trafficking in tobacco.

Once a prisoner got his hands on some tobacco, his problems were not over. Up to the 1920s, prisoners were expected to chew, not smoke their wad. Female prisoners were given snuff.

Those who insisted on lighting up anyway had to do a lot of improvising. Matches were hard to come by and many prisoners relied on "punk boxes".

The punk box kit consisted of a small box containing the punk (carbonized cloth), a flint-like stone and a "zipper" — a small metal disc with a string threaded through holes in the centre. The

zipper was spun against the flint, which cast off sparks. If all went well, the sparks ignited the punk which would light the cigarette. Around the turn of the century, prisoners fashioned home-made lighters from metal cylinders with interior spark wheels to ignite the punk.

By the 1920s, convicts at Kingston Penitentiary were allowed a weekly tobacco ration of one and a third ounces. The supply of cigarette papers was cut off, supposedly after the Warden surprised two convicts shooting craps and recording their bets on the papers. After this incident, inmates had to roll their smokes in toilet tissue. The "no papers" rule endured for a decade.

After the riots at Kingston in 1932, the rolling paper allowance was reinstituted and the tobacco ration was marginally increased. By 1934, well-behaved medium-security prisoners were allowed to smoke in the common rooms in the evening.

By 1935 prisoners were allowed to buy extra tobacco out of their five cents a day allowance. Even at Depression prices, this did not leave much for candy and magazines. Inmates today can purchase tobacco from a canteen without restriction, provided they have sufficient funds from their earnings. Tobacco continues to play a significant role in the prison barter system.

TIMES CHANGE

Within the penitentiary routine, the human dimension was often forgotten. But the exercise of strict controls did not snuff out all attempts to achieve a degree of normalcy. Roger Caron recounts his unsuccessful effort to have some fudge made by an unlikely chef, Alonzo Boyd, who for many years was Canada's most notorious bank robber. In Kingston Penitentiary at the time, Boyd "was making fudge; he had two pounds of fudge for me. He comes out to the yard where I am working in the weight pit and gives me two big cloth bags full of this square fudge with nuts in it. It was superb. At four o'clock the bell rings and I am going into the yard. You had to march single file and you weren't allowed to talk. I was going across the yard wearing my jojo — that was our winter coat. It was bulging a little bit. Keeper Hammond singled me out with that crooked finger of his: 'What you got in there? Open the coat.' There was my cloth bag with two pounds of fudge. He took it from me and I was almost crying. I was just dreaming of getting to my cell and getting that fudge. It's been thirty years now and I will never forgive him to my dying day. I know the guards ate it later. They thought it was funny. I thought that was the cruelest thing ever done to me in my whole life."

Kingston Penitentiary remained very true to its image most of the time. It was a sober, serious and secure institution, symbolized by its imposing entrance, solid high walls and searching towers. The contrast is all the greater when these grey stones are festooned with bunting, flags and colourful decoration, a gaudy transformation

that takes place at unscheduled intervals, such as on Dominion Day 1927, the sixtieth anniversary of Confederation.

Times change and so do social attitudes, none more so than how people see and think about crime. The set routine of a great penitentiary must be founded within the society which it serves. As society changed, the maintenance of the regimented penitentiary routine became increasingly less desirable. The penitentiary began a process of change, of opening up to society, of lessening the strictures on day-to-day life. The rules of association were relaxed. Inmates were permitted to become part of the process of operating the penitentiary.

But as these changes took place, the old discipline that had imposed order came under attack. The process of change was often difficult, with unexpected consequences.

CHAPTER IX

OVER THE WALLS, THROUGH THE GATE,
OFF ON HORSEBACK

OVER THE WALLS, THROUGH THE GATE, OFF ON HORSEBACK

It is estimated that at least 25,000 convicts have done time in Kingston Penitentiary. Very few have ever escaped, although a fair number have tried, and virtually every one has thought about it. Prison is not a nice place to have to stay. It was never meant to be. It was meant to be a place that people would want to stay out of. No inmates are there because they want to be. It is axiomatic that the first job of a penitentiary is to hold offenders who are there against their will. It is expected that some inmates will try any means possible to get out. The odds are heavily stacked against them.

WALKAWAYS

But nothing is impossible, and the dismal prospect of the prison dungeon has inspired more than one imaginative escape and creative attempt. Some have been spectacular and violent, involving injury and loss of life. Some have been what those who work and live in prisons call "walkaways". Inmates outside the walls, working on the farm or a construction gang or out on a day pass, often have the opportunity. Sometimes it coincides with an especially strong urge, like spring fever in the young. They simply down tools quietly, turn left and walk off. It usually is not long before the escapee is recaptured, stripped of his trusted status or work assignment and often handed some extra time for his trouble.

Walkaways are not always peaceful, of course. The first guard murdered at Kingston Penitentiary, Henry Trail, was the victim of two prisoners who had been working beside him at the lime kiln in the quarry. It was July 7, 1870.

Convicts Daniel Mann and John Smith struck Trail and killed him, took his coat, watch and pistol, and fled. The rest of the population was locked up immediately and every officer who could be spared was sent after the escapees. They were recaptured less than two weeks later.

The prospect of repeated incidents of guards losing their weapons to escapees caused authorities in later years to decree that officers in physical contact with prisoners should not carry guns.

The escape judged least possible, and therefore most dramatic, is from the Main Cell Block once the penitentiary is closed tight for the night and all inmates have been counted and locked in their cells. Nevertheless, it has happened.

Regardless of the means and no matter how daring, an escape sends waves of concern through the community. A violent escape by notorious criminals will attract massive police, press and community attention. In the past, the net of hot pursuit by penitentiary staff and local police has been cast widely. Penitentiary officers join the search until those unlawfully at large are recaptured. Not infrequently the trail leads to the

U.S., which is just on the other shore of Lake Ontario and the St. Lawrence River. The river and the lake meet at Kingston. There are the Thousand Islands of Gananoque to hide among if an escape is made by water. In 1923, the notorious Red Ryan gang led a senior penitentiary officer south of the border, and not everybody came back alive.

THE FIRST ESCAPE ATTEMPTS

The first attempted escape from Kingston Penitentiary was by convict Number 50, Alberzy Nakusilio, who managed a brief excursion on October 24, 1836. He secreted himself in the prison exercise yard sometime before the final lock-up, hoping to leave after officials were convinced that he was long-gone. He was discovered early the next day climbing over the fence, which was just a wooden barrier at the time, a matter of great concern to everyone responsible for keeping the convicts in custody. After a short pursuit, 50 was recaptured. He was given seven lashes in front of all the convicts assembled, and thrown in irons for months. Warden Smith took the opportunity to rail against the inadequacy of the plank fence and call for immediate construction of a real prison wall, too tall to climb, too thick to breach, with lookout towers to survey the entrance, yard and cell blocks. But the massive wall that surrounds Kingston Penitentiary today, often strengthened and rebuilt but still based on the stone cut and fit by the first inmates, was not to be finished for another ten years.

The first female convicts to escape were not long behind. On December 17, 1839, Emmie Whitting and Rhoda Morrison escaped from the female cells. The Matron, Mrs. Parsons, allowed

Morrison to lock herself and others, including Whitting, into their own cells. They seized their chance and readily escaped, the first escape from inside the cell blocks. The next day the Warden recaptured the two in Kingston, acting upon information received from local citizens, for which he paid one hundred dollars. That was a handsome sum for the day, so Warden Smith must have wanted them back very badly. Their fate is not known precisely, but it is believed that Emmie Whitting and Eunice Whiting, "the

beautiful girl of twenty" who caught the eye of Charles Dickens when he toured the penitentiary in 1842, were one and the same. Warden Smith chose only to remonstrate with Mrs. Parsons over her want of care. She kept her job.

THE WALL BRINGS A MORE SECURE FEELING

The completion of the permanent wall in 1845 brought a more secure feeling to the Warden and the community at large. Times were such that there was often more concern for intrusion by radical elements than for the threat of escape. It was not many years since the War of 1812, and such as it was that conflict had involved Kingston as much as any locale in Canada. There were rebellions and various upsets in both Canadas in 1837, led by Mackenzie in the west (Ontario) and Papineau in the east (Québec). When Lord Durham arrived from England for a five month look at the colonies in 1838, a look that would result in his famous **Report on the Affairs of British North America** and lead to the union of Upper Canada West with Lower Canada East in 1841, "the gaols," according to historian Donald Creighton, "were full of political prisoners."

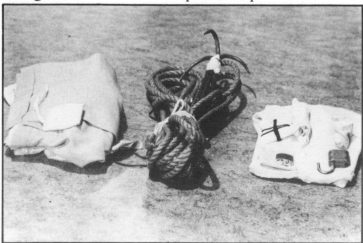

Tempers would be short and emotions run high in Canada for more than another generation. The Parliament buildings in Montréal were burned in a night of rioting in April 1849. In the next two decades the Fenians would be raiding from across the U.S. border, trying their dubious strategy of winning freedom for Ireland by guerilla warfare and propaganda in America. Thomas D'Arcy McGee would be assassinated on Sparks Street in Ottawa in 1868. A guard at Kingston Penitentiary was dismissed on evidence that his wife frequented a bookstore that carried Fenian tracts. They were turbulent years for the colonists who were trying to build a great nation. And to those who thought it ludicrous that anyone would try to break *into* Kingston Penitentiary, there was one persuasive reply. It had already been done.

BREAKING IN

It had not been done by rebels or revolutionaries, or relatives of those inside, but by a former convict. It was ten days before Christmas in 1857. Thomas Hardy had been released just two weeks before, at the end of November, after serving three years. He was only sixteen. Perhaps inspired by seasonal cheer, for he acknowledged that drink was a cause of his troubles, Hardy brought a ladder to the wall by moonlight and propped it on a log pile. Then, as the Warden later surmised, "being an active man he must have reached the summit by a spring."

But the rope he used to let himself down inside the wall became unfastened. He could not climb back out after he had rifled the cash box in the clerk's office, which is what he had come for. Attempts to build a ramp left him exhausted and the morning light overtook him. He took shelter

$50 Reward!

Convict Jean Baptiste Bienvenue escaped from a Quarry Gang at the Kingston Penitentiary on Monday afternoon, 11th September.

The Convict is 21 years old, stoutly built, 5 feet 2 in. high, fair complexion, brown hair and grey eyes, much sun-burnt, and has the style of a sailor

A Reward of $50 will be paid for his return to this Penitentiary.

JOHN CREIGHTON,

Kingston Penitentiary, 12th Sept., 1876.   Warden.

under some straw in the stable, but was soon discovered. For his effort, Hardy got six months which he served in the local jail. When he was released on July 31, 1858, he asked to see the Warden at Kingston Penitentiary. Apparently he wanted back the coat he had left behind during the break in. The Warden scolded him and told him to leave town. Hardy did just that. He sailed away by boat, never to be seen again.

THE CURIOUS AND TRAGIC CASE OF DR. DILL

The Warden's Journal for June 29, 1863, has as an entry, in the usual laconic form, the fact that Dr. William Dill died at 8:00 p.m. at the age of sixty two. Thus ended the tragic career of a brilliant but flawed medical practitioner. Dr. Dill's criminal career eventually drew in many of the leading politicians of his time and his own escape to a brief freedom shattered the innermost security of Kingston Penitentiary.

Dr. William Dill, the son of an Irish minister, had the education and upbringing to make him a leading light in the society of Canada West. Upon coming to Canada, he practiced medicine in the bustling community of Dundas, then the enterprising rival of nearby Hamilton. His skills were essential to the community and he attended to his medical practice with zeal and devotion.

But he had a strong will and temperament, bordering on arrogance. He despised the Tory hierarchy in the community and would not suffer fools gladly. He was, therefore, shunned by the local establishment. In early 1849, he began to treat Phoebe Fordham of Ancaster. In the course of this treatment, he found himself accused of rape by the girl. In a courtroom packed with twelve hundred people, Dr. Dill was found guilty and sentenced to death, as rape was then a capital offence. Upon hearing the verdict, Dr. Dill exclaimed, "My Lord, I am not guilty of this crime. Had I been guilty, I would not have stood here this day. I would have escaped."

In May 1849, his sentence was commuted to life and he was transferred to the provincial penitentiary at Kingston. Prisoner 2568, Dr. William Dill, was initially a model prisoner. However, the tight discipline and stark life of prison worked against his proud and rigid temperament. Soon his name began to appear in the discipline books. It was usually for minor acts of insolence, making faces, singing or shouting. But he proved a difficult and distant prisoner. Indeed, his mental stability was in question after the first few years. When he sought to be transported, in 1854, he was turned down. The Attorney General, John A. Macdonald of Kingston, advised the Cabinet against such mercy. When Dr. Dill was informed of this decision, he became a desperate man.

He began to plot his final attempt at freedom. He watched the guards and assessed the weak ones. He watched the routine within the prison. He secreted away the seemingly innocent pieces of metal, small keys and other items he would need. He sought out the security weakness — the ladder casually left, the nightly routine of a guard who might read his newspaper rather than do his rounds. Such is the enterprise of all those who seek to escape. They have the ultimate instrument to do this—time.

The prison was crowded and understaffed, six hundred inmates and thirty five keepers and overseers in all. It was easy for Dill to make his assessments. He worked in the cabinet shop, one of the ideal locations to this day to acquire tools,

where he could build what he needed and secret it away. Slowly he made his plan. He chose his guard well.

The keeper of the watch, John Mace, was inexperienced. It was he who would lock Dill's cell for the night. He did not know that the bolt was barred from flying into its hold by a piece of metal. Because he was new to the job, the odd sound that this makes would not signal a problem to him. On Saturday night, September 20, 1856, Dill stood at his barrier holding it shut as required. The key was turned in the normal way. However, it did not lock because of Dill's metal stop. He was therefore free to go onto his range.

Officer Meacle, more fastidious in snuffing the wicks of the kerosene lamps burning on the range than observing inmates, let himself onto the range, leaving the barrier open. Then, by great luck but with even greater danger, Keeper MacRae came onto the range to speak to Meacle. While they spoke, Dill left his cell and hid in the Main Dome. He slowly followed MacRae on his rounds until he met the one guard on the perimeter—there were no others.

The young guard, John Kennedy, was to remain in the employ of Kingston Penitentiary for more than fifty years, even though his career almost ended that evening. The plan fell into place quickly. Dill had secured two ladders, which he fastened together to reach the top of the wall. He had stolen a small amount of money from the cabinet shop. On a moonless night and with the perimeter guard pouring over the British Whig, Dill went over the wall and fled toward Kingston. He had secured an overcoat, but had to throw away his readily identifiable prison pants. He rushed to Kingston and boarded the mail boat bound for Ogdensburg, New York. It was as if it had been waiting for him.

Dill was able to find employment in this bustling community as a carpenter, a trade he had learned within the walls. But all was not right. As is so often the case with escaped convicts, his escape plans had not progressed to what to do with his freedom. Within a week he became homesick for his family. He knew that he could not stay away from his home country and slowly build a new life. In an act more foolhardy than wise, he applied for and got a job as a teacher in the village of Prescott across the St. Lawrence River from Ogdensburg, a scant seventy miles from the penitentiary.

In Prescott, he quickly attracted the attention of the townsfolk, one of whom had recently left the employ of the penitentiary. This man had heard of the escape and knew of the £100 reward. By October 2, just three weeks after his escape, Dill was returned to Kingston Penitentiary. For his efforts, Dill was chained and given "an infliction of four dozen lashes with the cats."

Dill's escape caused changes in the patterns of security procedures of the penitentiary that last to this day. Henceforth, no guard was to patrol a range at night unattended. The main barrier to the dome area was to be locked behind him by another guard. All ladders were to be secured with chains.

His mind weakened and his hope gone, Dill degenerated over the years. He continued to be punished regularly, once for "staring at the warden and biting his lips while the warden was visiting the cabinet shop, showing an expression of some evil desire at the appearance of the warden."

During the remainder of Dill's sentence, there were two further petitions by his family for a pardon. They originated in the belief that he had been wrongfully imprisoned by an evil conspiracy between his alleged victim and the local magistrates eager to rid themselves of this vexatious character. These pleas were, however, to no avail. This was the end. The years had taken their toll on this proud and arrogant man. The prison routine and grinding discipline continued to take its toll. And so, even as his family attempted another petition for pardon, he became ill and died.

ESCAPE FROM THE DUNGEON

The twenty five foot barrier with turrets increased the odds against inmate escapes, but it could not eliminate them entirely. Throughout Kingston Penitentiary's history there have been several. They are always a blow to Warden or staff, who make recapture their first priority. Warden Creighton, like his predecessor, offered rewards for the return of escapees.

Similarly, Warden MacDonell records a letter received from one Benjamin Wilson, offering complete details about his escape. The letter was posted from the relative safety of Boston. It appears that contact had been made previously. The escapee was writing once again with more details about the role of certain staff members who cast a blind eye while the fugitives managed to get over the wall, across to Wolfe Island and into the United States in short order!

There is no longer a dungeon or "hole" at Kingston Penitentiary. Troublemakers are sent to disassociation cells (diss cells), which are above ground in a concrete bunker located between the north and east wings running from the Main Dome. There are twenty diss cells. The occupants are confined twenty three hours a day, and take their hour of exercise alone in a segregated yard.

[Handwritten letter facsimile]

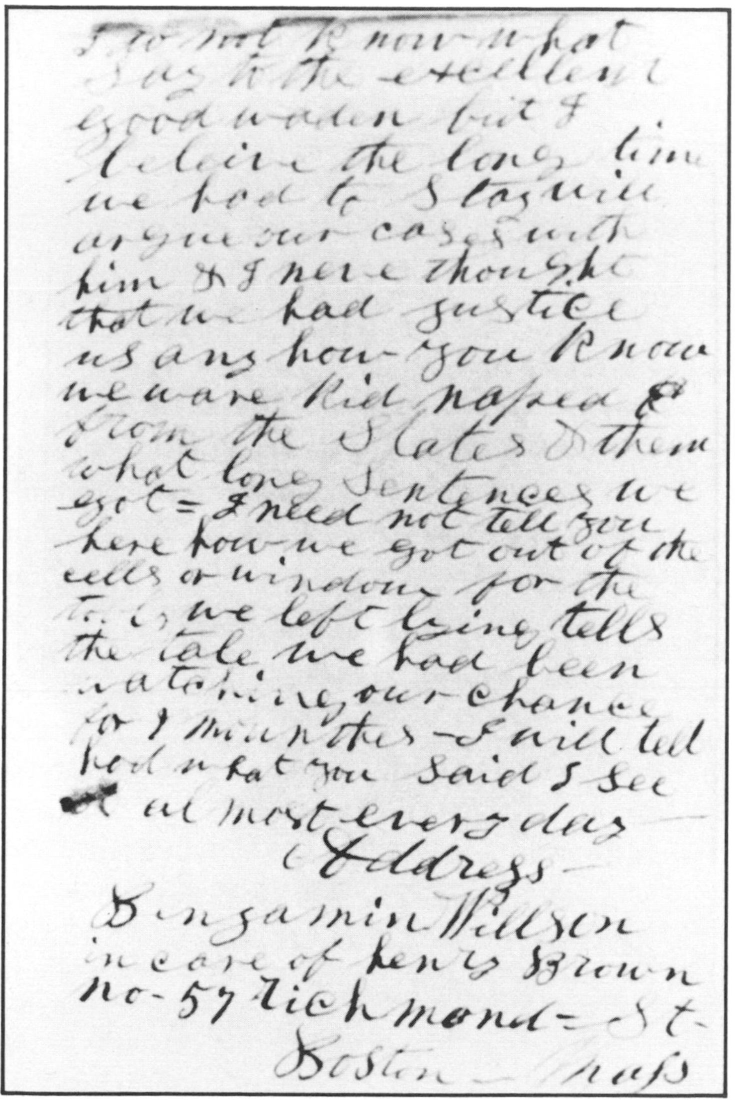

> I do not know what
> say to the excellent
> good warden but I
> believe the long time
> we had to stay will
> argue our cases with
> him & I never thought
> that we had justice
> us any how you know
> we ware kid napsed &
> from the States & them
> what long sentences we
> got — I need not tell you
> here how we got out of the
> cells or window for the
> to is we left lying tells
> the tale we had been
> watching our chance
> for I mean others — I will tell
> him what you said I see
> & at most everyday —
>   Address —
>   Benjamin Wilson
>   in care of henry Brown
>   no — 57 Richmond — St —
>   Boston — Mass

But in 1875 there was a dungeon, and anybody in it was fortunate to get an hour of exercise a week. Warden Creighton writes in his journal that he sometimes went in on Sunday to let convict Maurice Blake out for a while, a kindness that was to be repaid with a jab in the groin (see Chapter IV). But he did not go on Sunday, October 3, 1875. There were three prisoners in the hole that day. Blake was thought to be insane because of his irrational attacks on officers, and particular care was taken in his pres-

ence. John S. Smith had threatened personal violence and shown contempt for prison rules by talking during meals. He had been two months in the dungeon, since August 2. James Butler had been discovered cutting the bars in his cell on September 13 and "in view of his bad acts and expressed diabolical intentions" had been sentenced to three dozen lashes with the cats and solitary confinement afterwards.

Convict Blake was not involved in the escape, except insofar as he had the undivided attention of the officers whenever they came to the hole. Their caution with him may have distracted them from the others, at least that is what the Warden surmised. Certain it is that someone slipped Smith some tools with which he broke a hole in the arch of his cell, moved the flagstone on top of it and clambered out. He picked the lock on Butler's cell, then the lock on the outer door, slipped through a sawn bar on the window and out into the yard.

It had been a stormy day and the night was dark and windy. The watchmen had checked the hole at eight p.m. and all was well. They were supposed to go every two hours, but they skipped the count at ten and midnight. When they went back at two a.m., Smith and Butler were gone. Once out of the dungeon they cracked the carpentry shop to get ropes and ladders. Then they broke into the tailor shop. Each took a new suit of clothing intended for convicts about to be discharged. They went over the wall at Tower Four in the southwest corner. "A short ladder and two poles lashed together were the means by which they had reached the top of the wall and a piece of

sash rope hanging outside showed their way of descent to the ground again."

Convict Smith was not heard from again. Convict Butler was caught in December and returned to Kingston Penitentiary, where later he would incite other convicts to riot with the hope of escaping, but unsuccessfully. Convict Blake was released from solitary in February 1876 and promptly renewed his attacks on officers. He was in the dungeon again five years later, in February 1881, when another breakout from the hole was accomplished. This time he went along, with three others. They were all recaptured two days later.

The guards on duty the night that Smith and Butler escaped were found asleep at their posts less than a week later and were dismissed.

One novel form of escape was on horseback. In September 1914, convict Czymoindski stole a horse from the prison farm and escaped, following a route up Division Street in Kingston, into the McAdoo Woods north of the city, where he abandoned the horse. This was the same route followed by the Ryan gang in 1923, leading some to speculate that there was only one contraband copy of the local Kingston map circulating among inmates. Convict Czymoindski was later recaptured in Copper Cliff, Ontario.

THE ESCAPE OF RED RYAN

"Officials rushed to the North Gate, the bell was rung and very soon a posse was in hot pursuit." With these words, the Kingston Daily Standard began its story on one of the most famous escapes from the penitentiary. Norman "Red" Ryan led a group of convicts over the wall on September 10, 1923.

Ryan was serving twenty five years for armed robbery. In the company of four others, all

city. Warden Ponsford and his men followed in their own car. It was an early model, of course, and it picked this moment to backfire, then stall, and finally bring the hot pursuit to a sputter. The fugitives abandoned their stolen but reliable vehicle in the McAdoo Woods.

While rumours were rife that a mass escape was planned, the rest of the penitentiary remained quiet. The one exception was the women's prison, then housed in the Northwest Cell Block. Mrs. Vera Cherry who worked there at the time remembers how the female convicts rushed to their windows and cheered and yelled, causing a commotion heard outside the walls.

One inmate was injured and recaptured in the ensuing search. The rest escaped. Very soon Ryan was back to his old ways. With a new gang he was robbing banks in the Toronto area.

of whom shared long sentences and desperate attitudes, he set fire to the stable adjacent to the east wall. Under cover of the smokescreen, a ladder was raised to the wall and the five escaped. They left an inmate "trusty", who worked in the barn, tied up outside the building. Armed with a pitchfork, Ryan assaulted Chief Keeper Matt Walsh who tried to stop him at the base of the ladder.

The escapees stole a car from the adjacent Richardson property and rushed north out of the

The search soon became an international event. Deputy Warden R.R. Tucker pursued Ryan into the United States. Through contacts in the penitentiary, he was able to trace and observe his movements. The flamboyant side of Ryan could not long contain itself. He wrote Chief Keeper Walsh apologizing for hurting him. He might have known that sooner or later he would be back in the keeper's care again.

It was a mystery how the convicts got out of the area and avoided the broad net cast for them, eluding police and penitentiary staff. But word of how it was done got back to inmates via the prison grapevine. An informant finally let the Warden in on the secret a month after the escape. After abandoning the hot car and making their way on foot, the fleeing inmates had forced shelter and food from an elderly farmer living near Glenburnie, north of the city. Farmer Swift found the fugitives in his hayloft. Afraid of having his house and barn put to the torch, he gave them food and helped them on their way. He told no one for fear of reprisal.

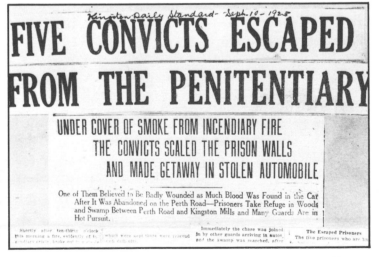

Kingston Daily Standard - Sept. 10 - 1925

FIVE CONVICTS ESCAPED
FROM THE PENITENTIARY

UNDER COVER OF SMOKE FROM INCENDIARY FIRE
THE CONVICTS SCALED THE PRISON WALLS
AND MADE GETAWAY IN STOLEN AUTOMOBILE

One of Them Believed to Be Badly Wounded as Much Blood Was Found in the Car After It Was Abandoned on the Perth Road—Prisoners Take Refuge in Woods and Swamp Between Perth Road and Kingston Mills and Many Guards Are in Hot Pursuit

Red Ryan was captured in Minneapolis on December 14, 1923, in a blazing gun battle with police. Ryan and his fellow fugitive, Arthur Brown, were ambushed when they went to collect a letter at a U.S. Post Office. Canadian and U.S. officers, and Kingston Penitentiary's Deputy Warden Tucker, had been waiting for them. In three months at large, they were suspected of a swath of bank jobs in Ontario, Iowa, Minnesota and Wisconsin. Ryan was wounded. Brown

managed to scramble away, but he was killed by police the following day. He had been fingered by a girl friend and caught by surprise at his boarding house.

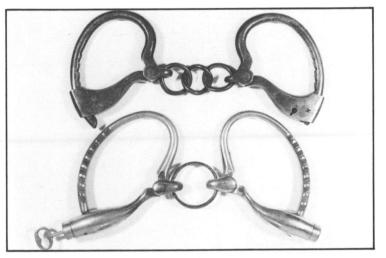

Ryan was returned to Canada and sentenced to thirty lashes and life imprisonment. He was a flamboyant manipulator, however, and his public notoriety brought him attention from the press and the public. Leading Canadians took up his cause and urged his release. Prime Minister R.B. Bennett visited Ryan at Kingston Penitentiary and declared that the man had been reformed. Red Ryan, alias Jack Slade, was paroled from Kingston Penitentiary in July 1935. On May 24, 1936, he was shot dead while robbing a bank in Sarnia.

ESCAPE FROM THE MAIN CELL BLOCK

One of the more notorious escapes from the Main Cell Block was on August 17, 1947, by Nicholas Minnelli, Ulysses Lauzon and Mickey MacDonald. Their cells were on the upper tier of H Range, which faces Tower One, the northeast Tower.

7-year robbery term, d was one of only two ~~ral months later h~~ nabbed in California. were never captured in a Mississippi dit~

They sawed through their bars and covered the cuts with wax and soot. There was not much that inmates could get in abundance in Kingston Penitentiary, but coal dust was readily available. The heating plant ran on coal for more than a century. On the night of the escape, this all-Canadian trio managed to get out of their cells and make it to the end of the range furthest from the Main Dome area, where the hub of security is strongest. They opened a barrier, climbed up to an attic, out of the building and over the wall. Minnelli later wrote all about it in a syndicated magazine article. He made it sound easy.

They left on the graveyard shift, after eleven p.m. and the final count of the day. All cells were locked and assumed to be secure. There were about a third as many officers on duty. Their planning was detailed and elaborate. It was several hours before the escape was discovered and the alarm raised.

They were less sure about what to do beyond the walls, though they did get out of Kingston for a time. Minnelli was recaptured after being stopped for drunk driving near San Francisco. When he wrote about his escape, he was writing from back in Kingston Penitentiary, where he was received with open arms on August 5, 1948. The daily count book notes a drop of one in the "At Large" column, and the laconic remark "Minnelle N. returned." Lauzon was found dead, also in the United States. He was struck from the "At Large" roster Sept. 15, with the notation "8343 Lauzon, off Count (Dead), effective August 1st, 1948." MacDonald never turned up again. He was presumed to have met the same fate as Lauzon, but no body was ever found. He remained an embarrassingly long time "At Large", until January 10, 1953, when the final notation appears in the keeper's count book "8213 MacDonald, Struck Off Register, Order of Commissioner." None of the three was at large for very long. It may not have been worth it. But they had done something that has been very rarely accomplished, before or since. They broke the main block of the big house.

ESCAPE WITH VIOLENCE

Some escapes occur with stealth and in darkness, others are open and violent.

John D. Kennedy was the prison messenger in 1948. He was a very popular officer and had a unique family connection to Kingston Penitentiary. He was born there, in an apartment in the West Gate. The gate, demolished in 1925, was at the centre of the west wall, where Tower Three rises, the only tower which is not at a corner of the penitentiary perimeter. John's father, Michael Kennedy, had held the prison messenger job before, during a career that started before he was fifteen and lasted for fifty one years. Part of that time he and his wife lived in the tower, where they raised eight children. Michael's brother John, the murdered officer's uncle, was also on the staff roster for more than half a century.

On the morning of April 26, 1948, John Kennedy agreed to give an inmate, Austin "Oscar" Craft, a drive from the penitentiary garage up to the North Gate. Unknown to Kennedy, another inmate, Howard Urqhart, was hiding in the trunk of the car, which the messenger was taking up to the Warden's house on the hill across from the North Gate.

The car was stopped in the passageway between the inner and outer gates when Craft got out and demanded the keys to the outer barrier. He had a gun that had been packed in earlier by a confederate. Kennedy refused and raised the

alarm. The convict shot three times. He took the keys to the front gate, unlocked the barrier and drove off. The car roared up King Street and into town. What ensued was one of the most concentrated manhunts in the history of the region. Police all over the province were alerted and descriptions flashed on the radio immediately. By one p.m. the same day, the escapees had been recaptured near the Village of Sydenham, northwest of Kingston. They offered no resistance.

Austin Craft was the last man to be put to death in the city of Kingston. He was hung in the jail behind the County courthouse. The last mention of him was made in the count book on October 29, 1948, "8899 Craft, Removed to County Jail, To Hang 24-1-49."

There was never an execution, nor a death row, at Kingston Penitentiary itself. The penitentiary is there to hold people with long sentences (two years or more). It was never a death house. While Canada practiced capital punishment, up until 1962 (it was not formally abolished until 1976), an inmate sentenced to death would be removed immediately to his place of execution, wherever it might be, usually a county jail. The

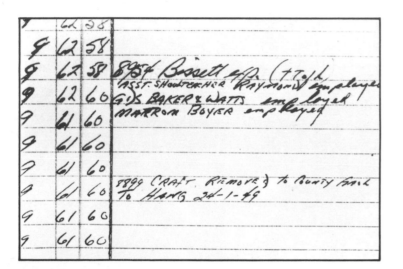

British North America Act of 1867 made the administration of criminal justice, including the administration of capital punishment, a provincial responsibility. This was true even when, as in Craft's case, the condemned man was already in Kingston Penitentiary.

BUILT TO ENDURE

Many efforts have been made to breach the bars, gates and walls of the penitentiary. Some have succeeded. Most have not. It has been suggested that the 1954 riot was an attempt to cover a mass escape. But no one got away then. The fact is that Kingston Penitentiary is a very secure institution. That, more than any other reason, is why it has survived so long.

There have been many movements to close it, starting with the proposed shift to Marmora in 1835 before the gates had even opened. Year after year in the 1920s, Warden Ponsford recommended that another penitentiary be built in a different location, citing overcrowding inside and the build-up of the city to the edge of the walls. Convicts on their way to farm and quarry were a danger to the citizens if they broke for freedom.

The authorities responded by doing away with farms and quarries so that the convicts would never venture beyond the gates.

Commissioner of Penitentiaries A.J. Macleod said in 1965 that the "out-dated" Kingston Penitentiary would be out of service by 1973. After the six-day riot of 1971 it was scheduled for mothballs (demolition would be prohibitively expensive) because of its age and the destruction of the ranges. But, like a "phoenix rising from the ashes", the big house was never entirely vacant and the ancient, damaged cell blocks were reconstructed slowly, almost imperceptibly. Two more wings re-opened in 1985,

leaving just two to be renovated before the institution would be whole again. Kingston Penitentiary is always reprieved, rebuilt and put to the uses of the day. It is simply too good a jail to close.

CHAPTER X

RIOT!!!

RIOT!!!

The word chills the blood of those who live and work in prison. Riot! For almost a hundred years Kingston Penitentiary was a fortress of security. It experienced no disturbance which could be classified as a riot.

A riot is generally a last resort by inmates to address a real or imagined grievance. During the nineteenth century major convict rebellion was virtually unknown, even though living conditions behind bars were far from perfect, far harsher than they are today. Obedience, order and silence were demanded. Corporal punishment was commonplace. The régime was oppressive, perhaps too strict even for the stricter standards of the day, but it was effective at stopping uprisings before they could start.

Not every incident is an escape attempt, nor every disturbance a riot. But every breach of security is treated with the utmost seriousness and resolve. In March 1985, on the eve of Kingston Penitentiary's hundred and fiftieth, three inmates managed to overpower four nurses and an officer. They held the hostages for seventeen hours in the prison hospital before being taken by the penitentiary's emergency response team. There were no casualties. A year earlier an inmate was shot and killed when he barricaded himself in the paint shop with a hostage and threatened to blow the place up.

THE RIOT OF '32

A penitentiary is said to contain the ideal mixture for a bomb, with a strong casing enclosing mounting pressure. When frustration boils over, the perimeter explodes. The first such explosion at Kingston Penitentiary took place in

1932. It resulted in an extensive investigation, the Archambault Report, which was to uncover a startling chain of events, and raise serious concern about the conduct of administrators at the penitentiary.

The disturbance resulted in a great deal of media attention, largely because of the involvement of Tim Buck, leader of the Canadian Communist Party. Together with eight other known communists, Buck was serving a sentence of four years for sedition, under section 98 of the Criminal Code.

This section made it a crime to belong to any political party that advocated change by the use of "force, violence or physical injury." It was aimed at communists particularly, and anyone who even attended a meeting where a communist was speaking could be charged. There was much social unrest in the country. These were the years of the Great Depression, the Dirty Thirties. The government used section 98 to silence Buck. It did not foresee that the political activists would import their brand of unrest within the walls.

The inmates had decided to stage a demonstration on the afternoon of October 17, 1932, to bring certain grievances to the attention of the administration. These included a request for cigarette papers (they received tobacco, but no papers) and more recreation. Their plan was to leave their place of work at three p.m. and gather in the yard.

But Acting Warden Gilbert Smith learned of the plan and had the doors to the workshops locked while the convicts were still inside. Those in the mailbag shop managed to climb out of a window, obtain an acetylene torch and cut the locks from the doors of the other shops. The population began to gather in the Main Dome. This is the great circular passageway from which all the cell wings jut out, like spokes from the hub of a wheel. It is the control centre for the whole institution.

In the dome, they addressed their complaints to the Acting Warden and asked that he telephone headquarters in Ottawa. His response was to call the military for assistance. To this point, the demonstration had been relatively peaceful. It probably would have remained so, had the military not been called in.

When the inmates learned that soldiers were on their way they crowded into the mailbag shop, taking some officers with them, and barricaded the door and windows. Shots were fired into the room either by a soldier or a guard. Several sewing machines used to work the heavy canvas bags were shattered. Subsequently, A/Warden Smith met with a committee of inmates and promised to take their complaints to Ottawa. Everyone returned to their cells without further incident.

But this was not to be the end of it. During the next few days, tension continued to escalate. On the afternoon of October 20, some convicts began to demonstrate in their cells, "busting up" in the prison vernacular. The army was again called out. Troops arrived from Canadian Forces Base, Kingston, within a few minutes and took up positions inside the penitentiary grounds. Penitentiary officers generally are not armed unless stationed at an armed post, such as the walkway overlooking the Main Dome area and all the cell ranges, known as Twelve Cage, or in a tower. But this day they were issued with rifles, revolvers and shotguns, and ordered into the ducts between the cells. Through the peepholes there inmates could be observed and counted whenever there was a requirement. There is no privacy in prison. The officers had orders to fire through the peepholes into those cells where convicts were continuing to cause a disturbance.

During the evening and night of October 20 the situation became more and more confused. Though all inmates were locked in their cells, many shots were fired. One convict took a bullet in the shoulder, and remained in his cell for twenty two hours before receiving treatment. Tim Buck testified, and his evidence was corroborated, that at least seven shots were fired into his cell. Miraculously he escaped injury. Many cells were damaged. A/Warden Smith was relieved of his duties and replaced on October 24 by Lt. Col. W.B. Megloughlin, M.C., who would be Warden for the next two years.

Many questions were raised in the House of Commons about how and why a mild demonstration had escalated to the point where guns were fired and life endangered. In February 1933, a 20,000-name petition demanding the repeal of section 98 was presented to Prime Minister Bennett. In November 1934 Tim Buck and his comrades were paroled. He left defiant, as he had arrived. A condition of his parole was that he was not to speak in public. The night of his release he addressed a large and jubilant crowd at Maple Leaf Gardens in Toronto.

THE RIOT OF '54

It was more than twenty years before anything similar broke the penitentiary peace, such as it is. But the disturbances of 1954 constituted a much more sinister intent on the part of inmates. Subsequent investigations never established satisfactorily the cause of the fires that erupted two days prior to the actual riot, nor the intent of some of the inmates concerning escape. At the time, the population of the penitentiary

had reached almost a thousand inmates. The preceding eighteen months had witnessed a growing number of disturbances in American prisons. One newspaper reported a total of thirty one major outbreaks in United States prisons during that period. Prisons throughout North America were badly overcrowded and unrest was in evidence everywhere.

On Friday, August 13, 1954, a fire started in the attic above the living area in the Main Cell Block. Initially, they thought it was caused by faulty wiring. However, as evidence later showed, it was doubtful that such a fire could possibly

have erupted accidentally. One officer discovered paint and an abnormal accumulation of rags in the attic just prior to the fire. This has never been confirmed but the nature of the fire has caused suspicion over the years. Inmates interviewed after the events by various newspapers said that this was to be the prelude to a mass escape attempt.

The fire left the cells uninhabitable. Because of structural damage to the cupola of the Main Dome, it had to be demolished. The Main Dome today still serves as convict control centre for Kingston Penitentiary, but without a dome. It now has just a flat roof. Inmates were herded into buildings south of the main block, where shops were to be used as dormitories. Murray Millar, who had been hired as probationary guard just two months before, was told by a keeper to get in with them to observe and keep order. The door was locked from the outside. Millar survived to become superintendent of the CSC Staff College, which is located roughly where the early quarries were.

On Sunday, August 15, as the group was being let out, a cry was heard. "Let's go." Officers were struck and, very quickly, up to twenty five

separate fires had been set in the shop area. This was followed by two hours of frenzied destruction and rampaging at the south end of the institution. It took the arrival of the army, which this time was called in with good reason, to quell the disturbance.

The rampage might have been worse but for an individual act of heroism. An unarmed twenty-three-year-old guard defied the rioters. Leslie McCallum was in the south area, in the Shop Dome, with a set of keys. When he saw what was happening, he pulled the barriers shut and locked himself in. The inmates raged about him. They threatened to burn him alive. He refused to surrender the keys. As smoke from the Main Dome fire got thicker and it grew darker, he managed to escape by donning an inmate's uniform over his own, opening the barrier and walking through the prisoners to the North Gate, where he was freed.

Warden Walter Johnstone had held his post only three months. He had taken over in May 1954 from Warden R.M. "Dick" Allan, whose twenty years as Warden had seen a creative flowering of inmate-organized activities, ranging from athletics to crafts to publishing. This

liberalized approach was to be continued by Warden Johnstone, even though he was welcomed by the worst riot he had seen since joining the Service in B.C. in 1934. The inmates had destroyed their work locations. They were immediately set to work rebuilding their prison, as their predecessors had done originally. They reconstructed the shops and other damaged areas. The high dome over the Main Cell Block, a Kingston landmark for over a century, was removed and the new flat roof installed.

Public reaction to the 1954 riot was generally very critical of the inmates responsible. Warden Johnstone's characterization of the ringleaders as psychopaths was generally accepted. However, the agenda was set for discussing correctional reform, overcrowding, the need for work and a classification system which would segregate the more dangerous offenders.

THE RIOT OF '71

The longest and most violent riot ever to take place at Kingston Penitentiary brought press and public reaction aplenty. On the evening of Wednesday, April 14, 1971, six inmates over-

powered an officer as they were moving back to their cells from the recreation hall. Within a few minutes, six guards had been taken hostage, and the Main Cell Block was in the hands of the inmates. There were six hundred and forty one inmates in the population, including fourteen who were in a segregated range, classified as requiring protective custody. During the next three days protracted negotiations were undertaken with the authorities. The captive officers

were dressed in inmate clothing and moved frequently, both for their safety from the more extreme rioters and to confuse would-be rescuers. The military was called in and took up positions around the cell blocks as they had done in 1932 and 1954.

While negotiations were underway the cell blocks were being smashed. Virtually every movable item was destroyed. The walls themselves could not stand against the pent-up rage and violence. On some ranges, iron and steel locking mechanisms were twisted and ripped from their bolts and tracks. Walls so thick that an arm would not stretch from one side to another were pummeled through with sledgehammers.

In the early morning hours of the fifth day, Sunday, some inmates broke into Range 1D, where the "undesirables" were held, and pried open the cell doors.

This horror was too much for many of the rioters, who quickly surrendered to waiting guards and troops. All day Sunday they filed out of the cell blocks after releasing their unharmed hostages. They were loaded onto buses and driven the short distance to the new maximum facility west of Kingston near the village of Bath — Millhaven Institution. It looked as though Kingston Penitentiary might be out of business for some time. It turned out to be not very long.

1835   1985

The occupants — child abusers, sex criminals, informants — were dragged into the centre of the Main Dome area and tied to chairs in a circle around the notorious bell. While the remainder of the population watched from the galleries high above, the fourteen were beaten and brutalized during the night. When it was over, one inmate was dead. Another died a few days later.

CHAPTER XI

KINGSTON PENITENTIARY TODAY

KINGSTON PENITENTIARY TODAY

The 1971 riot only hastened the inevitable.

For many years before, various announcements of the closing of Kingston Penitentiary had been made. At the time of the riot, the finishing touches were being put on its replacement — Millhaven. Staff were routinely warned. "The joint is closing."

It was not to be. With the opening of Millhaven, Kingston Penitentiary was to become another kind of place.

After the riot, Kingston Penitentiary was transformed into the reception centre for the Ontario region. Internal changes were made to reflect this new role. A new floor was built to reduce the number of tiers, or levels of cells, from four to two (they had been reduced to four from the original five in the previous renovation of 1885). In this way, accommodation was made less austere, providing more range space for inmates to congregate in. Everyone sentenced to federal penitentiary in Ontario was to be admitted here

for processing and classification, before being transferred to one of the institutions in the region. While at the reception centre, they would receive diagnostic and vocational testing to determine what trades or treatment would help to reduce the likelihood of their return to crime upon release.

The need to classify inmates and separate them into groups with roughly similar characteristics had been recognized from earliest times, when young and old, male and female, healthy and insane, violent and harmless were all confined together. Successive wardens, chaplains, surgeons and inspectors pleaded for a system that would allow offenders with like characteristics to be held together.

They urged a system that would relieve a first offender from having to serve his time, cheek by jowl, with habitual or hardened criminals. The peaceful or resigned prisoner should not be incited by the violent. It was bad for discipline and order. It reduced whatever hope there might be for rehabilitation.

The authorities did not pay much heed. It took thirty years to relocate lunatics out of Kingston Penitentiary and into Rockwood. It was more than seventy years until a separate prison building for women was erected. But through the late nineteenth and early twentieth centuries, as new penitentiaries were built, rudimentary classification came about in practice. Convicts too hard to handle at St. Vincent de Paul or Dorchester or in the west were simply transferred to Kingston Penitentiary.

Penitentiaries proliferated to cope with criminals as Canada's population exploded. From just over five million at the turn of the century, the population nearly tripled to more than fourteen million Canadians in 1950, aided by a singular surge of immigration. From 1910 to

1914 more than one and a half million immigrants were admitted to Canada, a number that had never been seen before and has never been matched since. More people led to more crime, which eventually resulted in the construction of more buildings to hold those who were convicted. It became feasible to design and build different types of facilities, geared to the known propensities of inmates.

In January 1984, CSC changed its security designation of maximum, medium and minimum

to a numerical system based on a scale of 1 to 7. Generally, community correctional centres are S-1; minimum security institutions, farms and forestry camps are S-2; medium security institutions range from S-3 to S-5; and maximum security institutions from S-6 to S-7. Multi level (M/L) means the institution houses several levels of security. Kingston Penitentiary is classified M/L.

During its stint as a reception centre in the Seventies, only a small number of "permanent" inmates were kept to operate essential services. Because of this, fewer cells were needed. Many were left untouched from the days of the riot, a spectacular reminder of the furious destruction of which desperate men are capable. In 1980, a walk through one unoccupied upper range revealed a newspaper lying on a cell floor. It was a copy of the now defunct Toronto Telegram, dated the first day of the 1971 riot.

ANOTHER CHANGE IN ROLES FOR KINGSTON PENITENTIARY

In the early 1980s parole officers were given responsibility for assigning prisoners to the appropriate institution. Only the Québec region maintained a reception centre. Convicted offenders elsewhere were now interviewed in provincial jails and a quick assessment made concerning the level of security required and the individual's program needs. This meant that the Correctional Service no longer needed a reception centre in Ontario. Kingston Penitentiary would be called on to make another shift in its role.

From the late 1960s and into the 1980s there had been a gradual change in the nature of

Canada's prison population. The emergence of the baby boom generation of Canadians, born between 1950 and 1965, meant a higher proportion of younger inmates. Youth is generally more explosive and less controlled in its reactions, particularly to confinement.

There were new and different offences involved. Child and sexual abuse cases were more vigorously prosecuted as public awareness of these crimes increased. Sex criminals, particularly those who violate young children, are on the

lowest rung of the prison hierarchy, despised by other inmates.

There was also a new drug culture in evidence. In 1967, there were almost a thousand convictions in Canada that were specifically related to drugs. This was the highest number that had ever been seen. The previous high of eight hundred drug-related convictions was in 1922. But by 1969 the number had leapt to 3,338 and five years later, in 1974, drug convictions had multiplied almost ten times, to 30,485. Not all of these convictions resulted in sentences of two years or more, which brings time in Kingston or another federal penitentiary, but some did. The convict code that once kept a semblance of decent behaviour behind bars began to crumble under an onslaught of swaggering, devil-may-care gang members and drug dealers with a taste for violence. There was no inmate ethic for them. The prison hierarchy or social structure began to collapse. This new breed of inmate was unpredictable, many were dangerous. Some were informants who could not be trusted by inmate or officer.

ESCAPE OF THE SPIRIT IF NOT OF THE BODY

The demon drug of the day has always been intertwined in the life of Kingston Penitentiary. After sin and idleness, drink was the most frequently cited cause of the behaviour that brought criminals to the North Gate. For well over fifty years each convict on discharge was subjected to a list of exit questions. Put by the chaplain, these were designed to discover what the convict thought about his treatment at Kingston Penitentiary and why he had landed there. Drink and drunkeness led all other self-appraisals.

Given the circumstances of the questioning not too much reliance can be placed on the candor of replies. But there is further anecdotal evidence supporting the link between drink, drugs and criminal activity. Articles abound on the subject in **Telescope** and other penal publications. Inmates in Kingston Penitentiary at times have published their own version of an Alcoholics Anonymous magazine, called **Aurora.**

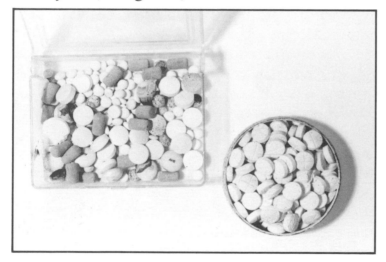

But there is more to the connection between doing drugs, of which drink is still the most common, and doing time. In a normal society, drink and drugs are used to relax, relieve tension and make time pass more pleasantly. In the penitentiary environment such relief is even more desirable. It is another form of escape — of the spirit if not of the body. But by the nature of the place it is forbidden. Recreational drugs are out — unless, of course, the inmate can find a way to get them in. Thus is set up the longest-running cat and mouse game in the history of Kingston Penitentiary. Inmates use all their ingenuity to build crude stills and keep them hidden until the mixture reaches potency. They are also looking constantly for accomplices who will pack drugs

in, usually amphetamines or hashish oil, which are easily concealed.

It is hard to hide a still and many are discovered by officers in the course of their rounds. They are usually destroyed on the spot. On occasion the brew might be adulterated with a diarrhetic. The distiller and his clients will be caught with their pants down the next day. Pills or hash oil are harder to find. Friends and visitors who are willing to pack them inside the gate know that they risk a frisk. A penitentiary "mule" will take great pains to conceal the contraband, often inserting it in a body cavity.

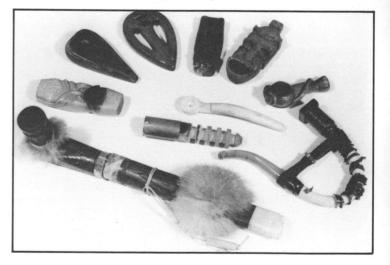

Mood altering substances become available sporadically, when a fast still goes undiscovered, or someone packs in pills. Nothing can be kept for very long or it will be uncovered by routine or non-routine sweeps, which can escalate very quickly to include a complete shutdown and a cell-by-cell, inch-by-inch search. Whatever the inmates get is ingested quickly. The result can be overdose. Instead of a tranquilizing effect, a psychotic state is induced, frequently a violent or suicidal state. This is what officers fear most about drugs. They are not taken recreationally at Kingston Penitentiary. They lead to ugly scenes.

People get hurt. In 1984, a valium-fuelled mass mania left a stack of mattresses so soaked with the blood of attempted suicides that they had to be discarded. Murray Millar observes that "you'll see more black eyes on guards than inmates at Kingston Penitentiary." Often enough drugs are involved.

PROTECTIVE CUSTODY

For whatever reasons—age, drugs, sexual deviance—there was a dramatic increase in the number of inmates requiring protective custody in penitentiaries across the country in the 1970s. Kingston Penitentiary was one of the institutions designated to conduct an experiment. Instead of having a segregation unit at each penitentiary, all protective custody inmates from across Canada would be brought to Kingston, Prince Albert, or Laval (formerly St. Vincent de Paul). These penitentiaries would become segregation units. Inmates who had been isolated from others for their own protection were to have all the privileges and programs available to inmates in an ordinary penitentiary. A second look was taken at Kingston Penitentiary cells that were still out of commission from the 1971 riot. Some were

modernized and reopened. As the hundred and fiftieth anniversary passed, only two trashed wings remain to be rebuilt.

MODERN PROGRAMS, PRODUCTS AND SERVICES

With a renewed mandate and a growing population, Kingston Penitentiary regained its maximum position in the correctional panoply, one that it had never lost for staff, inmates and the citizens of Kingston. Work programs were expanded. The mailbag repair and canvas shops were increased in size, continuing the tradition

begun in the 1870s. Many new vocational and industrial programs were added. The Information Processing Shop represents a new and growing phase of inmate employment. Direct descendants of the quarry, contract and factory operations of early days, Kingston Penitentiary industries now are incorporated in CORCAN. CORCAN is a registered trademark which identifies all the products and services provided by the federal penitentiary system. Kingston Penitentiary is now a minor part of the CORCAN network of almost a hundred plants in institutions from coast to coast. Eight thousand inmates were employed in 1983 at farms, forestry camps, industrial and information processing shops. The industrial shops manufactured more than five hundred products with a sales value of about $10 million. A hundred years earlier the total value of penitentiary production was $125,000, of which Kingston Penitentiary contributed almost half. Apart from expansion and diversification,

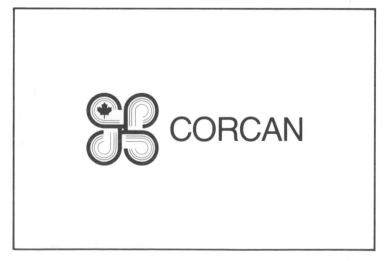

CORCAN continues and improves another important innovation. Inmates are now permitted to keep some of their earnings. In 1981 inmate pay scales were adjusted from a maximum pay level of $2.30 a day, to a minimum of $3.15 and as much as $7.55 per day depending on the job and the security level of the institution.

As well as earning, learning would be re-emphasized at Kingston Penitentiary. A new school program was introduced that covered the full spectrum of educational opportunities, from remedial reading and math upgrading to business administration and data processing.

As the population edged above five hundred there was a steady improvement in the buildings and accommodations. In the winter of 1985 a new heating plant was fired up, built near the old Warden's quarters, just below P4W. All construction projects on and around the property are attuned to the historic character of the buildings and the uses to which they are still put. Security comes first. From the tradition of the big house, Kingston Penitentiary maintains its emphasis on discipline and order. But out of the destruction flowed an era of reform which has provided many opportunities for inmates who are willing to change.

1835 1985

KINGSTON PENITENTIARY
NOW

A COLOUR PHOTO ESSAY

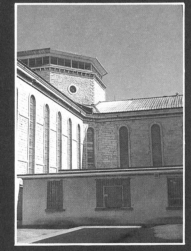

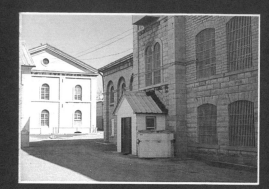

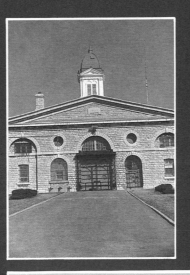

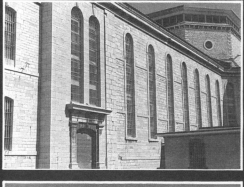

EPILOGUE

This book is not an epitaph to Kingston Penitentiary. The institution is still very much alive and serving as part of the modern Correctional Service of Canada. But this story has shown, if anything, that Kingston Penitentiary has been many institutions over the years. It has served many purposes, reflecting the uses to which confinement has been put by succeeding generations.

The buildings themselves are history. More importantly, the people who have lived and served within the vast walls of the institution are its story. They are its life.

It is very easy to treat human tragedy in a morose way. Indeed, one should not be flippant about the fact that individuals are punished for their crimes, that people are hurt by those crimes or that within the walls of the penitentiary there is also violence and frustration. But to dwell on these without reference to the basic humanity of the lives lived out within these walls is to do a very great disservice to the dedication of the staff and visitors from the community and to those who have been forced to make a meaningful life for themselves even after they have fallen into error. For those who work within the correctional field, it is always the essential strength of human hope in the most dire situations that shines through in the end.

And so, as Kingston Penitentiary turns not to the past but to the future, the journey through this very human environment ends where it began, at the North Gate, the main gate of the penitentiary.

NAMES AND NUMBERS

Warden's Garden, 1911

Warden's Residence, Side View   *View From Widow's Watch, Warden's Residence*

WARDENS — 1834 - 1985

Provincial Penitentiary (1834-1867)

Kingston Penitentiary (1867-1985)

—————1834—————
Henry Smith

—————1848—————
Donald Ae. MacDonell

—————1869—————
J. M. Ferres

—————1871—————
John Creighton

—————1885—————
Michael Lavell

—————1896—————
J. H. Metcalfe

—————1899—————
J. M. Platt

—————1913—————
A. G. Irvine

—————1914—————
Robert R. Creighton

—————1920—————
J. C. Ponsford

—————1932—————
W. B. Megloughlin

—————1934—————
R. M. Allan

—————1954—————
Walter Johnstone

—————1960—————
D. McLean

—————1962—————
V. J. Richmond

—————1966—————
Hazen Smith

—————1967—————
A. Jarvis

—————1972—————
J. Phelps

—————1972—————
D. Clark

—————1975—————
M. Nolan

—————1978—————
S. Scrutton

—————1981—————
Andrew Graham

—————1984—————
Mary Dawson

MENU FROM THE 1880s

In the Canadian penitentiary of the nineteenth century, 'coarse diet' was considered to be part of the punishment. This was a typical daily menu for men in the 1880s:

BREAKFAST

1 pint pease coffee (sweetened with 1/2 oz. brown
   sugar)
1/2 lb. brown bread
1/2 lb. white bread or 1/2 lb. potatoes
1/4 lb. beef or pork
(with beets and vinegar twice a week)

DINNER

1-1/2 pint soup
1/2 lb. white bread or 3/4 lb. potatoes
1/2 lb. brown bread
1/2 lb. beef, mutton or pork

SUPPER

10 oz. white or brown bread
1 pint coffee (with 1/2 oz. brown sugar)

Females had a lighter workload, so their food allowance was smaller:

BREAKFAST

1 pint of tea (sweetened with 1/2 oz. brown sugar)
1/2 lb. white bread
1/2 lb. brown bread

DINNER

1 pint soup
1/4 lb. brown bread
1/4 lb. white bread or 1/2 lb. of potatoes
3/8 lb. beef, mutton or pork

SUPPER

6 oz. white bread
1 pint tea (with 1/2 oz. sugar)
or
1/2 gill (1/4 pint) molasses
vegetables in season (with pepper, salt and vinegar)

Official attempts to add a little variety to prison meals were controversial. At the turn of the century, hardliners were outraged by reports that prisoners had been given plum pudding for Christmas. Some people called for a return to the bread and water régime.

Unofficially, prisoners found their own ways of supplementing their rations. Food often disappeared from the commissary and the guard's mess.

One of the ways that convicts killed the taste of institutional meals was by quaffing homemade hooch, which they distilled from tomato juice, potato peels and other food scraps. Some tipplers who did not know their ethyl from their methyl risked death from wood alcohol poisoning. In 1923, inmates P. Kearney and J. Hitt succumbed to a shellac-based cocktail.

WARDEN'S DAY, 1847

I delivered the keys to the Guard Wallis at five o'clock. Saw Reverend O'Brien attend for Service for Roman Catholic Female Convicts who were to receive the sacraments. Mr. Murry came in good time for the bell ringing. I attended to the opening of the prison. Saw convicts proceed out with buckets and assemble successively on brick ground, return to cells with buckets and proceed to breakfast. Some noise in the dining room regarding the state of the oatmeal, but I could see nothing wrong with it.

After breakfast, took out the convict Carru in charge of Guard Johnston to see my cow which has been overfed by the stable men and will probably die.

I met Contractor Mills in the prison yard and he informed me that he was going to turn off ten additional hands on Saturday, the first. I also spoke to Mr. Mills of his having stated that I had snubbed him on all occasions. This is false. In fact, from his attempts to irregularities, I have found it very unpleasant to deal with him. Some are of the opinion that he cannot control his temper, which I am informed is vicious in the extreme.

The man Forrester, whom I had placed outside to watch the wood pile, saw a man enter from the East side, observed him standing for some time but he was too great a distance from him to ascertain what he was like.

At noon court, I sentenced the convict L. Potter to three dozen lashes with the cats and to be confined to the dark cells till further orders for very nearly succeeding in murdering another convict, Peltier. Dr. Sampson looked at this man later on and made the observation that it appeared to him that this convict is mentally deranged.

Inmate Barbering

Early Moulding Shop

Sentenced John Leeds to five meals bread and water punishment for telling a falsehood to the Surgeon, saying it was not his wish to be brought before him and did not know anything about it till the guard took him from his work. This convict has attended the Hospital every day for the last week for the purpose of scheming and this morning his conduct was quite insolent and he was talking all the time while at the Hospital although told several times to be silent.

Sentenced Paul Levesque to four meals bread and water and one night without bed for throwing his meal about at breakfast, saying it was not fit for anyone to eat. When spoken to by Guard Worlen, he made a series of obscene noises.

Sentenced J. Charbone to be secured by chain for secreting himself in the yard at the closing of the prison with a view to escaping from the prison and remaining concealed until found, to the great annoyance of the authorities of the institution. This is a most troublesome convict.

I attended to general office business after dinner. Looked to see the name of convict R.L. Roberts. I find that his time in the Ledger opposite his name is incorrect. It should be eleven years instead of seven. Had it corrected. Mr. Inspector Dickson came between three and four o'clock. I brought under his notice the convicts idle in Mill's shop. He said he didn't see what could be done as Mills was of such a disposition that demonstration with him may endanger the contract. Mr. Dickson made a memento to authorize advertizing for cord wood—tenders to be opened on the twelfth of May.

I attended to see convicts proceed to their cells. Mr. Murry reported all counted after closing of prison and inspection of shops. I later visited prison at nine o'clock, all then quiet. I released the convict Palger from the dark cell, being apprehensive that the night might turn cold and he being only a boy.

The evils of keeping convicts idle is exemplified in Walter McVey, one of eleven convicts thrown out of work by Mr. Mills, who commenced this day to cut up his shoes with an axe. I will not be surprised next week to see other acts of violence brought about by Mr. Mills unwarrantable conduct.

INSIDER WORD GAMES

Six is just another number in the outside world. Inside Kingston Penitentiary, six is a person or a warning.

To be anywhere near complete, a lexicon of prison terminology would have to include thousands of entries. The language of prisons is rich and basic, and above all fast. In the early days prisoners were not allowed to speak at any time. Brevity was essential when you had to try. It is also important to be quick if one is about to be caught at some forbidden activity, and in prison there are many things like that. A lot of standard prison jargon is known because it was so heavily used by Hollywood in the era of the gangster film. Gangsters frequently ended up in jail, after their fling with criminal living. Prison talk throughout North America, and in some cases the world, shares many common terms, including fish (new convict), screw (guard), kid (passive homosexual). It is hard to say where many of them originate, except that they are often generic to prisons and not specific to location. Some probably started at Kingston Penitentiary. Six may be one of them.

"Got you, six," is a greeting from the Tower guard to the keeper as he walks the yard at mid-shift, just before the last count of the day is taken at 11 p.m. Six times a day, from morning to night, correctional officers must count every inmate and report the total to Keeper's Hall. If it does not tally, they go back and do it again. And if it still is not right, the search starts immediately. The senior man on duty at night will usually be a CX-6, Correctional Officer Six. He is the keeper and the boss.

To "stand six" is to watch out for the boss coming. To "call six" is to warn of his approach. The inmates are always on the alert for authority, and any guard is "boss", but "six" has special meaning.

Looking In, North Gate

The Weather Outside Is Frightful

PENITENTIARY VISITORS

As closed as Kingston Penitentiary might seem, it is nonetheless open to a great many people. In the 1800s, most of the visitors to Kingston Penitentiary were tourists, who were curious enough to pay a fee.

In 1985, a staggering number of outsiders still visit the penitentiary regularly, although it is now considered off limits to the merely curious. Friends and relatives of inmates may visit between 9 a.m. and 10:45 a.m., and from 1 p.m. until 3:45 p.m. seven days a week. For some inmates, these visits are of the type one often sees in movies — the inmate and visitor on opposite sides of a screened enclosure. But "open" visits, where the family or friend sit at a table, are becoming more commonplace.

In November 1983, the most recent innovation in inmate visits began with the introduction of private family visiting. Inmates earn the privilege, through hard work and good behaviour, of spending up to forty eight hours with members of their immediate family in a well-equipped house trailer located within the walls. Inmates may live with their wives, mothers, fathers, children or other close relative within an environment that resembles more a hotel room than a prison cell. Here they can cook their own meals, play with the children, and do the daily household chores common to most people living outside the walls. Alcohol or drugs are, of course, strictly prohibited.

These three types of visits — closed, open and private family visits — involve an average of more than five hundred family members and friends each month.

In addition to the family members and friends who enter the penitentiary daily, there are no less than thirteen volunteer groups which meet regularly with inmates, usually in the evening hours. These groups include

Alcoholics Anonymous, art groups, music groups, Chamber of Commerce, the John Howard Society, Allied Indian and Métis Society, the Salvation Army as well as countless volunteers who are cleared to enter the penitentiary. The contribution made by these volunteers is as significant as their numbers and as varied as one would find in the community. For many inmates without family or friends, volunteers represent their only link with the outside.

1835 1985

HONOUR ROLL

1835 1985

Staff who have lost their lives in the performance of their duty at Kingston Penitentiary:

1) H. TRAIL -1870 - GUARD

2) D. CUNNINGHAM - 1890 - INSTRUCTOR

3) M.E. JENKIN - 1926 - GUARD

4) J.J. McCORMICK - 1936 - GUARD

5) J.D. KENNEDY - 1948 - GUARD

6) W.C. WENTWORTH - 1961 - GUARD

CABINET MINISTERS RESPONSIBLE
FOR
KINGSTON PENITENTIARY

1835 1985

ATTORNEYS GENERAL
UPPER CANADA
1834
Henry J. Boulton

1835
Robert Jameson

1837
C. A. Hagerman

ATTORNEYS GENERAL
CANADA WEST / CANADA EAST

1841
W. H. Draper / C. R. Ogden

1842
Robert Baldwin / L. H. LaFontaine

1844
W. H. Draper / James Smith

1847
H. Sherwood / W. Badgley

1848
Robert Baldwin / L. H. LaFontaine

1851
W. B. Richards / L. T. Drummond

1853
J. Ross / L. T. Drummond

1854
John A. Macdonald / L. T. Drummond

1856
John A. Macdonald / George-Etienne Cartier

1858
John S. Macdonald / L.T. Drummond
John A. Macdonald / G.-E. Cartier

1862
John S. Macdonald / L. V. Sicotte

1863
John S. Macdonald / A. A. Dorion

1864
John A. Macdonald / G.-E. Cartier

ATTORNEYS GENERAL OF CANADA

1867
Sir John A. Macdonald

1873
Antoine-Aimé Dorion

1874
Sir Albert James Smith

1874
Télesphore Fournier

1875
Dominick Edward Blake

1877
Toussaint-Antoine-Rodolphe Laflamme

1878
James McDonald

1881
Sir Alexander Campbell

1885
Sir John Sparrow David Thompson

1894
Sir Charles H. Tupper

1896
Arthur Rupert Dickey

1896
Sir Oliver Mowat

1897
David Mills

1902
Charles Fitzpatrick

1906
Sir Allen Bristol Aylesworth

1911
Charles Joseph Doherty

1921
Richard B. Bennett

1921
Sir Jean-Homer Gouin

1924
Ernest Lapointe

1926
Hugh Guthrie
Léon Patenaude
Ernest Lapointe

1930
Hugh Guthrie

1935
George Reginald Geary
Ernest Lapointe

1941
Joseph-E. Michaud
Louis St. Laurent

1946
James L. Isley

1948
Louis St. Laurent
Stuart Sinclair Garson

1957
Edmund Davie Fulton

1962
Donald Methuen Fleming

1963
Lionel Chevrier

1964
Guy Favreau

1965
George James McIlraith
Louis-Joseph-Lucien Cardin

SOLICITORS GENERAL OF CANADA

1966
Lawrence Pennell

1968
John Napier Turner
George James McIlraith

1970
Jean-Pierre Goyer

1972
Warren Allmand

1976
Francis Fox

1978
Jean-Jacques Blais

1979
Allan Frederick Lawrence

1980
Robert Phillip Kaplan

1984
Elmer MacIntosh McKay

1835 1985

KINGSTON PENITENTIARY

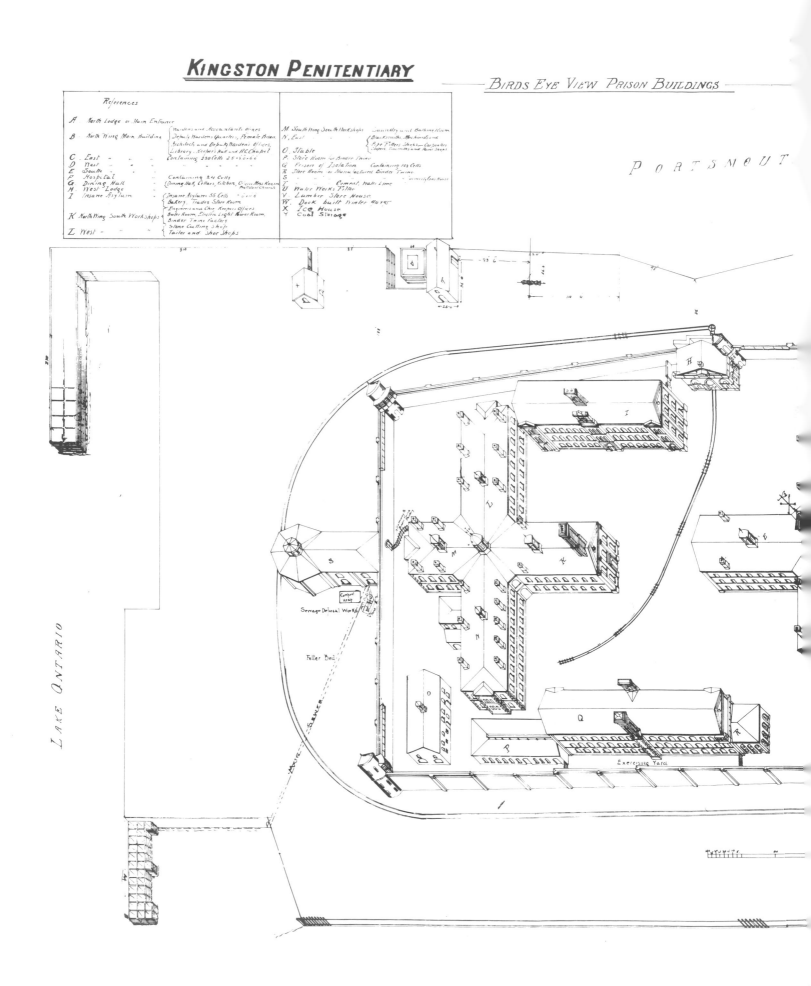

References

A North Lodge or Main Entrance

B North Wing Main Building
- Wardens and Accountants offices
- Deputy Wardens Quarters, Female Prison
- Architects and Deputy Wardens offices,
- Library, Keeper's Hall and R.C. Chapel
- Containing 280 Cells 2½ × 3 × 6.6

C East
D West
E South
F Hospital   Containing 24 Cells
G Dining Hall   Dining Hall, Cellars, Kitchen, Organ Mess Room
     Protestant Church
H West Lodge
I Insane Asylum   Insane Asylum 56 Cells
- Bakery, Trades Shoe Room
- Engineers and Chief Keepers Offices
K North Wing South Workshops   Boiler Room, Electric Light Power Room
- Binder Twine Factory
- Stone Cutting Shops
Z West   Tailor and Shoe Shops

M South Wing South Workshops   Laundry and Bathing Room
N East
- Blacksmiths, Machine Shop
- Pipe Fitters Shops, Carpenters
- Coopers, Tinsmiths and Paint Shops
O Stable
P Store Room for Binder Twine
Q Prison of Isolation   Containing 108 Cells
R Store Room or Manufactured Binder Twine
S
T   Cement, Slate Lime
U Water Works Filter
V Lumber Store House
W Dock built Winter Quarters
X Ice House
Y Coal Storage

PORTSMOUT

LAKE ONTARIO

Sewage Disposal Works

Filler Bed

Exercising Yard